How to Attract Hummingbirds & Butterflies

Created and designed by
the editorial staff of
ORTHO BOOKS

Project Editors
Nancy Arbuckle
Cedric Crocker

Writers
John V. Dennis
Mathew Tekulsky

Illustrators
Paul Kratter
Andrea Tachiera

Designer
Gary Hespenheide

Ortho Books

Publisher
Edward A. Evans

Editorial Director
Christine Jordan

Production Director
Ernie S. Tasaki

Managing Editors
Robert J. Beckstrom
Michael D. Smith
Sally W. Smith

System Manager
Linda M. Bouchard

Product Manager
Richard E. Pile, Jr.

**Marketing Administrative
 Assistant**
Daniel Stage

Distribution Specialist
Barbara F. Steadham

Operations Assistant
Georgiann Wright

Technical Consultant
J. A. Crozier, Jr., Ph.D.

Address all inquiries to:
Ortho Books
Chevron Chemical Company
Consumer Products Division
Box 5047
San Ramon, CA 94583

1 2 3 4 5 6 7 8 9
91 92 93 94 95 96

ISBN 0-89721-232-0
Library of Congress Catalog Card
Number 90-86168

Chevron Chemical Company
6001 Bollinger Canyon Road, San Ramon, CA 94583

Acknowledgments

Copy Chief
Melinda E. Levine

Editorial Coordinator
Cass Dempsey

Copyeditor
Hazel White

Proofreader
Deborah Bruner

Indexer
Shirley J. Manley

Composition by
Nancy Patton Wilson-McCune

Editorial Assistants
John Parr
Laurie A. Steele

Associate Editor
Sara Shopkow

Layout and Production by
Studio 165

Photo Editors
Sarah Bendersky
Ann Leyhe

Separations by
Color Tech. Corp.

Lithographed in the USA by
Webcrafters, Inc.

Consultants
Dr. Luis Baptista, California Academy of Sciences,
 San Francisco, Calif.
Dr. Paul Opler, U.S. Fish and Wildlife Service,
 Ft. Collins, Colo.

Special Thanks to
Louise Blakey, Los Altos, Calif.
Betsy Clebsch, La Honda, Calif.
Elizabeth Gamble Garden Center, Palo Alto, Calif.
Catherine Habiger, Menlo Park, Calif.
Bernard Jackson, Memorial University,
 Newfoundland, Canada
Scott Loosley, Palo Alto, Calif.
Bridget Makk, Menlo Park, Calif.
Bill Thompson III, Bird Watcher's Digest,
 Baltimore, Md.
Elsa Thompson, Bird Watcher's Digest, Marietta, Ohio
Craig Tufts, National Wildlife Federation,
 Washington, D.C.

Photographers
Names of photographers are followed by the page numbers on which their work appears. R=right, C=center, L=left, T=top, B=bottom.

Tim Brown: 74, 80
Earl E. Burr: 42
COMSTOCK, Inc.: 18, 68T, 89
Townsend P. Dickinson/COMSTOCK, Inc.: 23B
Jeff Foott: 8T, 17B, 28, 30R, 41, 65
Saxon Holt: 1, 4, 7BL, 10, 16, 21, 27, 30L, 34, 35T, 35B, 36, 38, 39, 40, 44, 48L, 48TC, 48BC, 48R, 49C, 49R, 50L, 50C, 50R, 51L, 51R, 52, 68B, 69BL, 69BR, 70T, 70B, 76, 77, 82TL, 82BL, 82R, 83L, 83TR, 83BR, 84L, 84R, 85L, 85TR, 85BR, 86, 88T, back cover TL, back cover BR
Bernard S. Jackson: 8BL, 54TR, 56B, 58R, 61T, 62T, 62B, 69T, 73, 75T, 75BR, 79, 81, 88B, 99TR
George O. Krizek, M.D.: 7T, 54L, 54CR, 56T, 58L, 64C, 64B, 66, 75BL, 100L, 102TL, 103R, 106R
Michael Landis/Ortho Information Services: 71R, 72T
George D. Lepp/COMSTOCK, Inc.: 9T, 13T, 14T, 24T, 24B, 47, back cover TR
Michael McKinley/Ortho Information Services: 33R, 78B
Anthony Mercieca: 4 (inset T), 8BR, 10 (insert), 17T, 22B, 25T, 25B, 32, 86 (inset T), 90L, 90R, 91, 93L, 93R, 94L, 95R
Dave Maslowski/Maslowski Wildlife Productions: 6TL, 6TR, 6B, 13B, 14B, 15, 19
Paul A. Opler: 4 (inset B), 9C, 9B, 29R, 54BR, 55C, 55B, 60T, 60B, 61B, 63T, 63C, 63B, 64T, 86 (inset B), 98L, 99L, 99BR, 100R, 101L, 101R, 102BL, 102R, 103R, 104TL, 104BL, 105R, 106L, back cover BL
Ortho Information Services: 72B
J. Parker/ Ortho Information Services: 31
Pam Peirce/Ortho Information Services: 71L
Mathew Tekulsky: 7BR, 78T
Michael S. Thompson/COMSTOCK, INC.: 33L, 68C
Luke Wade: 12, 22T, 23T, 26T, 26B, 92, 94R
E. N. Woodbury: 52 (inset), 96L, 96R, 97L, 97R, 98R, 101L, 104R, 105L

Front Cover
A Ruby-throated Hummingbird feeds from a phlox (*Phlox paniculata*). The butterfly above is an Eastern Tiger Swallowtail; the one below is a Monarch; and at left is the Melissa Blue.

Back Cover
Top left: Placed in a peaceful spot, this bench is an ideal location from which to observe hummingbirds in the surrounding sage shrubs.

Top right: A female Allen's Hummingbird perches between feeding flights.

Bottom left: Here, a Small (American) Copper, one of the most beautiful common butterflies, visits orange milkweed.

Bottom right: The ideal butterfly garden is full of color and a variety of nectar flowers; black-eyed-susan, yarrow, sedum, and anemone are shown here.

Title Page
An American Painted Lady visits a garden of zinnia and lupine.

How to Attract Hummingbirds & Butterflies

The Pleasure of Hummingbirds and Butterflies

People have gardens for many reasons—for the beauty of flowers, for the activity and challenge of growing flowers, and for the refuge that a well-planned garden offers. Many gardeners have taken gardening further, attracting hummingbirds and butterflies to complement the beauty of the flowers themselves.

Among the many types of birds, insects, and mammals that are attracted to gardens, hummingbirds and butterflies are perhaps the most appealing. They provide an element of active beauty to the garden and opportunities to observe their habits and brilliant colors. Together they display a full spectrum of color: Butterflies show blue, yellow, and white; hummingbirds, a wide range of greens, reds, violets, and black.

It is fascinating to observe the unfolding of their life cycles, and their interactions with plants. Nectar from the blooms of a wide assortment of annuals, perennials, shrubs, vines, and trees will attract both hummingbirds and butterflies.

In addition to their popularity, hummingbirds and butterflies also share a number of traits. Both possess marvelous powers of flight, have iridescent coloring, and obtain much of their nourishment from the nectar-producing flowers of plants.

Although hummingbirds resemble certain insects in some ways—sphinx moths are sometimes mistaken for hummingbirds—they have all the attributes of other birds. They build nests, lay and incubate

A well-planned garden can both lure hummingbirds and butterflies and be practical and attractive. This garden combines daisies, phlox, iris, sage, hollyhock, eveningprimrose, and other plants.
Inset: A male Black-chinned Hummingbird hovers while taking nectar.
Inset: A Monarch butterfly at a zinnia blossom.

Top left: A male Ruby-throated Hummingbird at a coralbells blossom, a favorite hummingbird flower.
Top right: The bright, iridescent gorget—as on this male Broad-tailed Hummingbird feeding at a desert-trumpet—is a unique, distinguishing feature of male hummingbirds.
Bottom: Butterflies lend color and movement to the garden. Here a Black Swallowtail takes nectar from a zinnia.

eggs, hatch and care for young, and share most of the behavioral characteristics of other birds.

Among birds, hummingbirds are most like their closest relatives, the swifts—fast-flying birds with long-pointed wings that obtain food by capturing insects in midair. Hummingbirds do the same, but they also obtain a large share of their nourishment from flowers—in the form of insects and nectar. The flower-feeding habit is responsible, in an evolutionary sense, for the resemblance that hummingbirds have to certain insects. Their bright color and dependence upon flowers show a closeness to butterflies; their flower feeding, swift flight, and general appearance, to sphinx moths.

For those who have flowers near their house or apartment, watching hummingbirds obtaining nectar can be a source of endless interest. Glittering color, swift flight, beauty, and grace make the scene as captivating as any that a garden can offer.

Butterflies offer similar viewing pleasures as hummingbirds and are also frequent garden visitors. They can be enticed into the garden by providing suitable plants for each of their life

A female Tiger Swallowtail taking nectar at butterfly weed.

Left: Hummingbird feeders provide an additional food source, but must be kept clean and filled. Place feeders at a safe distance from windows.
Right: Host plants provide essential food for butterflies at the larval stage of their development.

stages. Butterflies feed on certain plants during their larval stage and other plants during their adult stage. As a rule, they select a limited number of plants at each stage to meet their needs—leafy plants for the larval stage and plants with nectar-producing flowers of the right kind for the adult stage. A number of plant blossoms are well suited for the needs of both hummingbirds and butterflies.

DESIGNING THE GARDEN

Whatever the species of butterflies and hummingbirds that you attract to your garden, you can provide for them without compromising your other plans for the garden. You can plant hummingbird and butterfly gardens on a large or small scale in any number of styles. For example, simply decorating a gazebo with baskets of hummingbird and butterfly flowers or planting an urban window box with them could attract an American Painted Lady butterfly or a Broad-tailed Hummingbird to within viewing distance.

The reward for a carefully designed garden with a few of the right flowers might be seeing an orange and black Monarch alighting on a marigold or a Ruby-throated Hummingbird hovering at a honeysuckle vine. You might also see a Black Swallowtail taking nectar from a butterfly bush or an Anna's Hummingbird taking nectar at a bottlebrush.

Choosing the Right Plants

To help you select plants that will attract hummingbirds and butterflies, the following chapters contain charts of plants that are especially well suited for hummingbird or butterfly gardens. In addition to their powers of attraction, most of these plants are highly decorative and have other valuable features as well—some attract both butterflies and hummingbirds, others attract honeybees, and a number are fragrant. All have limits as to the region and kind of site where they will grow well, so consider your climate, soil, and the amount of sun and shade on your site as you make your selection.

In cold-winter zones, keeping plants indoors during winter will effectively extend the range of plants you can grow. In spring, when hummingbirds and butterflies arrive, you can move these plants to window boxes or the outside, where their blooms will furnish early season nectar and continue providing food throughout the summer.

Only one or two plants in a genus are listed in the charts. This does not mean that other plants belonging to the same genus are not equally well suited for hummingbirds or butterflies—check with a local garden center for species that will grow well in your area. In addition to the plant charts, each hummingbird and butterfly description in the last chapter (see pages 89 to 106) includes a list of favorite flowering plants.

Top right: Several favorite hummingbird flowers are North American natives, like this ocotillo. Here a Costa's Hummingbird takes nectar.
Bottom right: A female Calliope Hummingbird feeds her young. Nestlings are fed large amounts of tiny insects.
Bottom left: A butterfly garden must provide protected spots for roosting. Here a Clouded Sulfur seeks shelter from rain.

Meeting Other Needs

Not to be overlooked in planning a garden to attract hummingbirds and butterflies are such other needs as water, shelter, supplemental food supplies, and sunlight. Sugar water in special feeders is the best source of additional food for hummingbirds; some butterflies will feed on overripe fruit, sugar water, tree sap, fungus and other nonplant sources. Hummingbirds require insects as a protein source. Butterflies must have open areas in which to bask in the sun. Hummingbirds seek protected sites for their nests. Both need shelter from adverse weather and predators. A successful garden must provide for these needs to attract and keep hummingbirds and butterflies.

Having hummingbirds and butterflies in your garden will provide you with many hours of interest, enjoyment, and entertainment, as well as an invaluable connection to the natural world. For those who have not already become hummingbird or butterfly gardeners, the pleasures are great and the rules simple. The first step—beginning in the next chapter with hummingbirds—is to learn about the habits and needs of these fascinating creatures. In the following chapters you will be drawn into their remarkable world—and, through your efforts, they will be enticed into your garden.

A female Allen's Hummingbird rests between feeding flights.

Left: The eyespots on the Buckeye butterfly are a protective adaptation, serving to confuse predators. Bottom: The Mourning Cloak—like the one shown here basking in the sun—feeds on the sap flow of trees, especially oaks. It may also choose fermenting fruit as a food source. It is an infrequent nectar feeder.

Hummingbirds in the Garden

During the course of their evolution, humming-birds have developed an array of remarkable physical characteristics and behaviors, ranging from the color of their plumage to their extra-ordinary ability to turn, hover, and fly. By study-ing hummingbirds just a little, the home gardener can learn to both attract them into the garden and better enjoy their presence.

Hummingbirds have adapted their flight and feeding methods perfectly to the difficult feat of obtaining nectar from flowers. While hovering before a flower on rapidly beating wings, they insert their bills into the floral opening and withdraw nectar with a long tongue. Hummingbirds, in turn, serve as pollinators for the flowers they take nectar from, transferring pollen from one flower to another on their head plumage. Many of these plants have evolved ways to encourage hummingbirds and discourage other nectar feeders.

The hummingbird's rapid flight is similar to the flight of some insects, but is unique among birds. Instead of having wings with several movable joints, which other birds have, hummingbirds have only one joint at the shoulder, allowing greater flexibility and an upstroke as powerful as the downstroke.

Hummingbird nesting practices are very much the same as those of other birds. In keeping with their small size, hummingbirds build tiny nests and lay tiny eggs. The male, aside from inseminating the female, takes no part in domestic duties.

Placed in a peaceful spot, this bench is an ideal location from which to observe hummingbirds in the surrounding sage shrubs.
Inset: A male Anna's Hummingbird perches, his beautiful coloring in easy view.

This Blue-throated Hummingbird exhibits a splendid example of the brilliant coloring characteristic of hummingbirds.

The songs of some North American hummingbirds, although not especially pleasing to the human ear, are extremely complex. Hummingbirds make a variety of other distinctive sounds—the males produce high-pitched twittering notes, and the wings of many hummingbirds buzz when in flight. Sound effects, such as these, differ from species to species.

Because of their unique characteristics, hummingbirds have a special place in the animal kingdom. Studying their similarities to and differences from other birds and insects is rewarding, although for most people simply having them around is enjoyment enough. This chapter provides an overview of hummingbirds and their behavior and describes how to design a garden that will attract them and keep them coming back.

NAMES AND CLASSIFICATION

The early Spanish explorers, the first Europeans to encounter hummingbirds, were impressed by their swift flight, needle bills, brilliant colors, and small size. They gave them such imaginative names as *aves varias,* "many-colored birds," and *joyas voladores,* "flying jewels." The New England colonists—inspired by the buzz or hum the birds made with their wings when in flight—were the first to call them hummingbirds.

During the eighteenth century, when animals were given scientific names according to a simple system devised by Carolus Linnaeus, a Swedish naturalist, order was brought to the naming of birds. The hummingbirds were placed in a family of their own, the *Trochilidae.* The name comes from a Greek word, *trochilos,* meaning small bird.

The hummingbirds are divided into genera, one category below family in Linnaeus's classification system. Hummingbirds are so diverse in appearance and features that there are numerous genera—those birds that are closely similar to one another belong to the same genus. For example, the Ruby-throated Hummingbird of the East has a western counterpart, the Black-chinned Hummingbird. Both belong to the genus *Archilochus.* The species name serves to separate one kind of hummingbird within a genus from another. Colorful Latin names such as *Amazilia beryllina* (the Berylline Hummingbird) are matched by equally colorful common names: Lucifer, Magnificent, Calliope, White-whiskered Hermit, Violet Sabrewing, and Green-tailed Emerald. The names are in keeping with the awe and wonder that has always been attached to these gemlike birds.

DISTRIBUTION

Hummingbirds almost certainly evolved in northwestern South America before spreading northward into Central and North America and southward into Brazil. Today there are approximately three hundred and forty species of hummingbirds in total. Ecuador has 163, the largest number in any one country.

Of the 21 species that reach North America, 16 breed here, another is a regular visitor, and 4 others are regarded as strays—only occasionally present. Of those that breed, only 10 have ranges that extend a significant distance north

Hummingbirds, such as this female Rufous, have evolved the specialized flight and feeding skills necessary to obtain nectar from tubular flowers.

The Ruby-throated Hummingbird is the only hummingbird that breeds east of the Mississippi River. Some members of this species regularly migrate across the Gulf of Mexico to their winter range in Mexico and Central America.

of the Mexican border (see the gallery of North American hummingbirds beginning on page 89). Four of these ten species reach Canada, and one, the Rufous Hummingbird, breeds as far north as Alaska. The greatest traveller of all is the Ruby-throated Hummingbird, whose range extends as far west as Alberta, east to Nova Scotia, and south through the eastern United States. The Ruby-throated is the only hummingbird that breeds east of the Mississippi. To reach wintering grounds in Mexico and Central America, many Ruby-throateds fly across the Gulf of Mexico, returning to nest by the same route.

Except during migration, hummingbirds are not likely to be found in the Great Plains region of the United States and Canada. Only a single species, the Buff-bellied Hummingbird, breeds in south Texas. All the other North American hummingbirds have a more western distribution; the largest number is found in the mountainous regions of western Texas, New Mexico, and Arizona.

Top: The typical hummingbird egg is large in comparison with the laying adult female. Clutch size is small—usually two eggs are laid.
Bottom: Blind, nearly naked, and totally helpless when hatched, young hummingbirds, such as the two Ruby-throateds pictured here, soon acquire feathers.

LIFE CYCLE

Hummingbirds, in reproducing their kind, go through the same series of stages that other birds do. But there are differences in timing. For example, the Anna's Hummingbird, present in the Far West, is one of the earliest of all birds to begin breeding activities. Courtship rituals and nesting begin as early as December. Costa's and Allen's hummingbirds, with ranges in southern parts of the Southwest and California, respectively, begin nesting as early as mid-February. On the Palos Verdes peninsula of California, both species breed the year around.

Mating

The hummingbird nesting season gets under way with elaborate "sky dances" performed by the male. These differ somewhat from species to species. One of the most spectacular displays is that of the Calliope Hummingbird, the smallest of all North American hummingbirds. At the beginning of the nesting season, the male Calliope, rising to a height of 60 to 90 feet, suddenly dives toward the ground, and transcribing a wide arc, rises once again to approximately the same height. The bird makes a loud whistle at the bottom of the dive. The performance may be repeated three or more times in rapid succession and is used partly to impress the female and partly to ward off males of the same species and other birds as well. In most hummingbird species the male continues to perform these dances throughout the nesting season and sometimes longer. Females sometimes conduct similar aerial performances.

In spite of his attentiveness during courtship, after having inseminated the female the male moves on. He takes no part in nest building or in the rearing of young birds.

Nesting

The typical hummingbird nest is very small, usually only 1½ inches in outer diameter. It is cup shaped, lined with plant down, and held together with spiderwebs. Many hummingbird species anchor their nests to the tops of horizontal tree limbs, where they look like a natural protrusion. Some nest in vines, on large fern fronds, on hanging rope, and even on light fixtures. Hummingbirds usually place their nests where overhead shelter offers some protection.

In some species, notably the Rufous and Calliope hummingbirds, the female often builds her nest on top of the one she built the year before. As many as four such nests, representing four consecutive years of nesting, have been recorded.

Laying Eggs and Rearing Young

After building a nest, a chore that may take about a week, the female lays two, sometimes three, pure white eggs. The eggs of all species are elongated in shape and are tiny, averaging about ½ inch in length—large in comparison with the small size of the parents. Eggs are incubated for approximately 15 to 17 days, depending upon the species.

As with this immature Ruby-throated Hummingbird, the coloration of juvenile hummingbirds of both sexes resembles that of the adult female.

The newborn birds are featherless—aside from two rows of downy plumes on their backs—and blind during the first few days after hatching. The young remain in the nest for about three weeks. Toward departure time the nest often becomes too small to hold the growing youngsters and they perch on the rim.

One brood is typical in most species, but the Allen's and Rufous have two broods per season and the Anna's and Black-chinned as many as three. Species that have more than one brood begin nesting early in the year and have their last brood in late summer or early fall.

Through a variety of survival adaptations, including torpidity (see page 18), hummingbirds have evolved to be quite long-lived. In the wild they have been known to live as long as five years. Ages of nine, ten, and fifteen years have been recorded in hummingbirds held in captivity.

Flowers specifically adapted for pollination by hummingbirds tend to discourage insect pollinators because of their structure, color, and lack of fragrance. Fuchsias, rich in number of blossoms as well as nectar, are a hummingbird favorite.

FOOD REQUIREMENTS

Hummingbirds are extremely active birds with high calorie requirements. To maintain their rapid metabolic rate, they must feed often and will visit hundreds of flowers during the course of a day. Flowers that produce a lot of nectar and produce it over a long period of time are far more helpful to hummingbirds than flowers that produce limited nectar. Especially useful are plants, such as the fuchsias, that produce numerous blossoms that are filled with nectar over much of the year.

Nectar From Plants

In many cases, the plants that hummingbirds depend upon for food are in turn dependent upon hummingbirds for their pollination. These plants evolved at the same time as hummingbirds, developing specific features that allowed hummingbirds access and excluded pollinators of other kinds. The flowers of these plants are tubular, scentless, brightly colored (often red), and easy for hummingbirds to hover before. Some flowers are shaped to accommodate hummingbirds with specialized

characteristics—such as decurved, very long, or relatively short bills.

Hummingbird flowers have protruding stamens tipped with anthers covered with pollen. As the hummingbird probes the blossom for nectar, some of the pollen brushes off onto the bird's feathers. When the bird visits the next blossom of the same kind, some of the pollen sticks to the stigma (female organ) of the plant. In this way the plant is fertilized. The hummingbird in turn is rewarded with a nutritional source—sips of nectar of exactly the right strength and sweetness.

Insects for Protein

Hummingbirds cannot survive on nectar or on sugar-water solutions (see Using Hummingbird Feeders, page 42) alone. They time their migrations to coincide both with the blooming seasons of favorite flowers and the presence of small insects. Hummingbirds visit flowers for nectar and for insects, an essential protein source. They capture spiders in their webs, insects that live on or inside flowers, and flying insects on the wing.

The long, narrow bill and tongue of the hummingbird enable it to extract nectar from tubular flowers. Here a female Calliope feeds from a hovering position.

Food Sources and Range Expansion

Some human activities unquestionably assist hummingbirds. One of the most important ones is providing garden plantings that supply hummingbirds with nectar and nesting sites. As population—and gardening—have expanded, so too have the ranges of some hummingbirds. In parts of the West, where wildflowers disappear with the coming of the dry season, the importance of yard plantings to hummingbirds can scarcely be overestimated. More and more people are offering hummingbirds not only nectar flowers but an extra source of food at sugar-water feeders. Something for birds to fall back upon when natural food is in short supply, and capable of furnishing the energy needs of hundreds of hummingbirds, sugar-water feeders are also having an important effect on hummingbird populations. Range expansion in the Anna's Hummingbird and several other species has coincided with the ever more widespread popularity of hummingbird feeding.

Sugar-water feeders provide an extra source of nourishment for hummingbirds, such as this female Blue-throated Hummingbird.

Hummingbirds are also attracted to the sap of trees, both for the sap flow itself and insects drawn to it. A female Calliope Hummingbird is pictured here.

TORPOR

Hummingbirds—along with swifts and night-jars, their two closest relatives—have the unusual ability to slow their bodily functions and go into a kind of trance or torpor. To maintain their high rate of metabolism (the highest of any warm-blooded animal, with the possible exception of the shrew), hummingbirds must feed every 10 minutes or so during the day. At night when the birds can no longer feed or during periods of stress, they slow their metabolism to conserve energy.

During periods of torpor the heartbeat slows from as many as 1,260 beats per minute to only 50 beats per minute. There are periods when a torpid bird does not breathe, is stiff and numb, and to all appearances, is dead. A hummingbird may remain in this condition overnight and for most of a day.

The ability to become torpid is of great survival value. Hummingbirds frequently become torpid at night, and when day comes they quickly revive. Hummingbirds found in a torpid condition during a cold day revive if provided with warmth and remain active as long as they can find food.

PREDATORS AND OTHER HAZARDS

Hummingbirds have few enemies. Their small size and quick flight make them poor targets for birds of prey. Seldom do hawks capture hummingbirds. Cowbirds, which disrupt the nesting of other birds, do not lay their eggs in hummingbird nests as they are too small. The small, well camouflaged nests of hummingbirds are also generally overlooked by nest robbers, such as jays and tree-climbing snakes.

Nevertheless, there are a number of ways in which an unwary hummingbird can suddenly meet its death. Their habit of hovering before spiderwebs either to prey upon the spider or obtain webbing for nest building exposes them to the danger of becoming entangled. There are occasional reports of hummingbirds caught in webs and unable to escape. Almost any small predator, such as a house cat, has a chance of catching a hummingbird if it lies in wait near their favorite flowers or bird feeders.

Hummingbirds, however, face potentially far greater dangers from the weather. Cold weather, prolonged rainy spells, dry weather that causes flowers to wither, and storms during migration are some of the hazards. Because these are risks that hummingbirds have always faced they have developed ways to compensate for them. For example, losses in the population in one year may be made up for by a good breeding season the next year.

The impact of the changing landscape and widespread use of herbicides and chemical sprays is hard to assess, but these factors could easily be adversely affecting hummingbird populations. Chemicals kill the small insects the birds feed upon and are potentially damaging to the birds themselves, since they are ingested through the nectar or from residues left on flowers.

VOCALIZATION AND DISPLAY

Although hummingbirds do not produce songs that are recognizable or appealing to humans in the way those of songbirds are, their vocal skills are considerable. Despite their simple vocal apparatus (the syrinx), hummingbirds are capable of learning very complex songs. Hummingbird songs are uttered so rapidly that the human ear perceives them as high-pitched squeaks, chirps, and twitters—although some tropical hummingbirds do have songs that are considered appealing by human standards. Because songs are learned, there are also identifiable regional differences among them.

In addition to their songs, hummingbirds also produce distinct wing noises. Wing noise is produced by air rushing through the feathers during flight. The male Broad-tailed Hummingbird, one of the most gifted of the wing instrumentalists, produces a musical buzzing sound with its wings as well as a cricketlike trill. The beating of the wings of the female Broad-tailed produces a humming sound. Male Rufous Hummingbirds produce a high-trilling buzz with their wings. Wing sounds are helpful in identifying different hummingbirds, especially if the bird making the noise is hidden from view.

Male hummingbirds perform spectacular aerial displays (see Mating, page 14) the year around. The display flights often take the form of U-shaped nosedives, during which the bird rises to a height, suddenly dives at a fast speed, and then zooms up again. In a second kind of display, the male flies back and forth in front of a perched female. His wings produce a whistling sound and his bill may be partially open.

Aerial displays are also conducted for the purpose of frightening away intruders that come near a nesting territory or food supply. These displays are often effective: To the intruder, the tiny hummingbird may seem like an attacking wasp or hornet.

Chimney Swifts, like hummingbirds, enter a sleeplike state of reduced body temperature and metabolism during the night or during cold periods.

FLIGHT

Their ability to make unusual maneuvers in flight sets hummingbirds apart from other birds. They are able to hover in midair, fly backward, forward, and reach high speeds. Their normal flight speed—between 25 and 30 miles per hour—is not extraordinary. But during a flight display, after gaining a height, a bird will suddenly dive and in some species reach a speed of 60 miles an hour.

Hummingbirds make long nonstop flights during migration; for example, the Ruby-throated Hummingbird's flight across the Gulf of Mexico. Although many birds fly as far and farther, journeys of this length were once thought to be impossible for birds this small. Powerful wing muscles and fat reserves that serve as fuel are the secrets behind this ability.

Hummingbird Display

With his bill pointed downward, (1) the male hummingbird rises high above the ground, (2) pauses, and (3) then dives almost straight down, making a dazzling swoop over the object of his display.

The hummingbird's flight skills are accomplished with the aid of very rapid wing beats. As many as 80 beats per second have been recorded in forward flight and 200 beats in display dives. These are faster wing beats than found in any other birds. The wings move so fast that they appear as a blur when the birds are flying or hovering before a flower. Hummingbirds have achieved a mastery of the air that combines the flight skills of both birds and insects.

ANATOMY

Many of the hummingbird's remarkable achievements relate to its unique anatomy. Its wing structure is unlike that of other birds and enables it to hover and to fly both forward and backward. The bill, too, distinguishes the hummingbird from other birds. It is uniquely adapted to the hummingbird's feeding habits. Also of particular interest is the extremely long hummingbird tongue, which is indispensable in gaining nectar from long, tubular flowers.

The Wings

Hummingbirds have long narrow wings that are propelled by muscles that make up 25 to 30 percent of their body weight. Instead of, as in other birds, wing bones that are flexible at wing joints, hummingbirds have rigid bones reaching to the shoulder. Although other birds can generate power only on the downstroke, hummingbirds—because of the way their wings are attached—can move freely in any direction.

The Bill

The bill varies in shape, length, and coloration from species to species. It is characteristically straight or curved downward, long, tubular, slender, and either black or red or a combination of the two colors. In one species the bill is curved upward. Hummingbirds that nest in North America have average-length bills that range from about ½ inch to 1 inch in length. The Plain-capped Starthroat, a Mexican species that occasionally strays across the border into the United States, has a bill that measures 1½ inches in length. Much longer bills are found in some South American species. The Andean Swordbill holds the record with a bill that measures up to 4 inches in length.

Hummingbird Anatomy

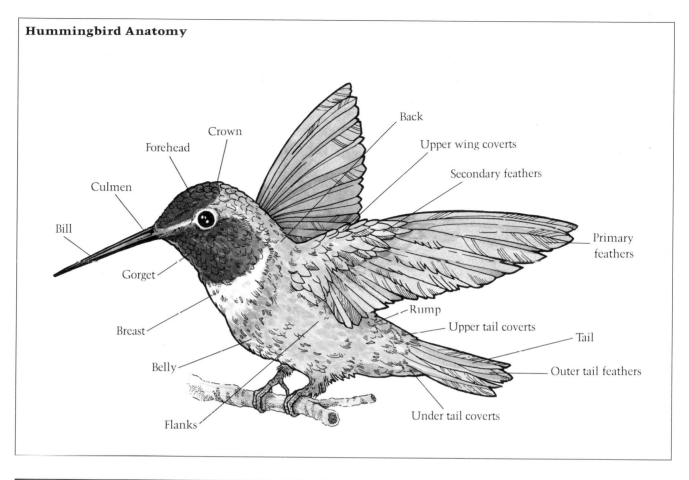

Hummingbirds, such as this Anna's nectaring at a sage, have a remarkable flight mechanism that allows them to hover for periods of significant duration and to fly backward at substantial speed.

Top: This female Black-chinned Hummingbird exhibits the hummingbird's unique wing structure. Bottom: Hummingbirds are distinguished by their long bills.

Bills of species that nest in North America are either straight or slightly downcurved (decurved). The bill of the Lucifer Hummingbird, which nests in the Chisos Mountains of western Texas, is the most decurved. The Buff-bellied, Violet-crowned, White-eared, and Broad-billed hummingbirds sport red bills with black tips; the others have black bills. As its name sug-

gests, the Broad-billed Hummingbird has a somewhat wider bill than found in other North American species. This is thought to be an adaptation for capturing insects on the wing. It is known that the Broad-billed is more of an insect eater than the other species. Besides using their bills as tools for probing flowers and catching insects, hummingbirds use them as weapons.

The Tongue

In contrast to butterflies, which normally spend five seconds or more at blossoms rich in nectar, hummingbirds spend only a fraction of this much time. If a blossom is unrewarding, a hummingbird recognizes this instantly and moves on to another. The hummingbird's ability to feed rapidly can be explained by the expert way it uses its bill and tongue when probing. As it hovers, it thrusts its bill into the floral opening and leaves the rest to the tongue. As specialized as any part of the hummingbird's anatomy, the tongue is deeply split at its tip, and also fringed in some species. The split portion of the tongue is folded into a tube when the bird feeds. Nectar is not sucked up but held in the tubular portion and swallowed when the tongue is returned to the mouth. After it has emptied the nectary of the flower, the hummingbird flies off to perhaps make the rounds of still more blossoms.

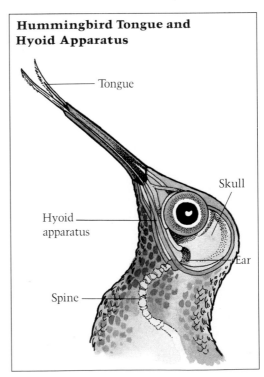

Hummingbird Tongue and Hyoid Apparatus

Tongue

Skull

Hyoid apparatus

Ear

Spine

Hummingbirds, such as this Blue-throated on lobelia, use their long tongues to collect nectar with a licking motion.

Hummingbirds are able to use their tongues so efficiently because of the way they are attached. Like woodpeckers, hummingbirds have a bony structure called the hyoid apparatus that serves to extend the tongue for considerable lengths and pull it back in again. The hyoid consists of two bony coils, one attached to one side of the base of the tongue and the other to the other side. The coils curve around the back of the skull to their respective places of attachment (except for the Magnificent, whose hyoid attaches behind the left nostril).

Hummingbirds are rewarded not only by the nectar they find in blossoms but also in some flowers by tiny insects that live in the floral tube. These are withdrawn by the tongue with the help of saliva, and, in some hummingbird species, the fringe of tiny bristles found at the edges of the tip of the tongue.

Deep-tubed nectar flowers that open in the daytime are primarily adapted for pollination by hummingbirds because of the long bills,

Both insects and nectar can be extracted from the floral tube.

The color of the gorget of this Anna's Hummingbird will change depending on how the light strikes it and from what angle it is viewed.

This close-up of the gorget of a male Anna's Hummingbird shows the iridescent feather tips.

correspondingly long tongues, and remarkable flying skills characteristic of hummingbirds. Thanks to their special adaptations, hummingbirds exchange their pollination skills for food swiftly and well.

PLUMAGE

Charles Darwin was so struck by the dazzling plumage of the hummingbirds he saw in South America that he compared them to the beautiful and renowned birds of paradise. He attributed their bright colors to sexual selection, females choosing more brightly colored males over less colorful ones. Although this explanation is correct as far as it goes, hummingbirds are colorful regardless of gender, and in some species the male and female look exactly alike.

Protective Color and Iridescence

It is not an accident of nature that most daytime nectar feeders, including hummingbirds and butterflies, are brightly colored. Their colors match the colors of the bright flowers they visit. This makes nectar feeders, as they visit flowers, difficult for predators to see. Protective coloration, as well as swift flight, make hummingbirds a poor target for birds of prey.

In keeping with their small size, hummingbirds have small feathers. The feathers are closely packed together but not interlocked by feather tips (barbules) as in most other birds. Hummingbirds have earned such epithets as flying jewels because of their iridescent colors. Iridescence is caused by the reflection of light upon minute air-and-melanin-filled feather structures called platelets. Depending on how the light strikes the platelets and the angle at which they are viewed, different color effects are produced. Thus, the colors of a humming-

Hummingbirds have long been sought after because of their brilliant plumage. The male Magnificent Hummingbird is among the most dazzling of species seen in North America.

The specialized feather structure of hummingbirds produces highly colorful plumage. The gorget of this male Rufous is especially distinctive.

bird's plumage are structural as opposed to the pigmented colors that are found in most birds. Nearly all of the hummingbird's feathers are iridescent, but some parts of the plumage are much more brilliantly colored than other parts.

Male and Female Plumage

The gorget, a brightly colored feathered area on the throat, is particularly brilliant in male hummingbirds. Depending on how the light strikes it, the gorget may appear intensively colored or almost black. A gorget that glows a ruby red most of the time can change to an iridescent blue, a metallic green, and a reddish purple before turning back to the original bright red. The colors change as the bird is viewed from different angles and in different light. On a cloudy day or when the bird is in the shade, the gorget, like the other plumage, may appear dark and without color.

In addition to colorful gorgets, males of many tropical species sport prominent crests, long tail streamers, and other adornments that capture the attention of the female during courtship. Although lacking finery of this kind, females are often brightly colored if compared with the females of many other bird species. They must not be overly visible to predators as they sit on their nests and go about their domestic duties. At the same time, like the male, they should blend in well with the flowers they visit. The compromise most often seen in female North American species is iridescent green above and grayish white or white below. Unlike the male, females in most species have white corners at the tips of their outer tail feathers.

Females are difficult to identify as to species. They have only a few plumage characteristics that are helpful in distinguishing one species from another. But size, length and shape of bill, and voice are useful clues. In contrast, adult males, with their bright colors, gorgets, and other markings can usually be identified with comparative ease if seen under good light conditions.

Young Plumage

Young, during their first few days in the nest, are featherless except for two downy rows on the back. The air movement from their mother's wings moves these feathers and alerts the young that their mother is near; they then beg

for food. By the time the young birds are ready to leave the nest, they are well feathered and resemble the adult except for a lack of iridescence. Before the first molt, which takes place at the end of the breeding season, young males have a mixed plumage, showing some characteristics of each parent. The young female, on the other hand, has a similar dress both before and after the molt. She looks exactly like her maternal parent.

Top: The brilliant coloring of male hummingbirds plays an important role in courtship display. Bottom: Female hummingbirds are less brightly colored than males so as to appear less visible when carrying out their nesting duties.

A HUMMINGBIRD GARDEN

Hummingbirds are present during some portion of the year in every part of North America except the far North and treeless plains. Moreover they fearlessly enter residential areas, where they nest near houses and obtain their food in yards and gardens. Like butterflies, they are attracted to flowers—some of them are special hummingbird flowers, others they share with butterflies and other nectar feeders. To have butterflies and hummingbirds close by and sharing the garden is something within the means of every gardener. Like the flowers that attract butterflies, most of the flowers that appeal to hummingbirds are ones also favored by gardeners.

The way to start attracting hummingbirds is to add a few more of the plants they like, especially those that have come to be called hummingbird flowers (see page 29). Arrange the plantings to meet the special requirements of hummingbirds. They should be highly visible and the flowers should be easily accessible to hummingbirds as they hover on rapidly beating wings. For a hummingbird garden to attain a reasonable state of perfection takes time and a certain amount of experimentation on the part of the gardener. With every year the garden will offer more enjoyment and attract more hummingbirds.

A second way of attracting hummingbirds is by providing them sugar-water solution in specially designed feeders. Feeding and planting for hummingbirds go hand in hand. Start with planting nectar flowers and go on to placing feeders. Once hummingbirds become accustomed to a yard, they come back year after year and usually in ever greater numbers.

Meeting the nectar demands of even a few hummingbirds requires many flowers and flowers that come into bloom at different times of the year. In some cases, this means a continual bloom from the time hummingbirds arrive in the spring until the last one departs in the fall. In other cases, a year-round blooming season is necessary. This is important in parts of the West where some species overwinter. Likewise along the Gulf Coast, where the Ruby-throated Hummingbird and a number of western species are now spending the winter in ever greater numbers.

The importance of having hummingbird feeders in addition to flowers cannot be overestimated. Even flowers with the longest blooming seasons and most copious nectar supplies may not be able to fully furnish the nectar needs of hummingbirds. Not only do feeders supply unlimited quantities of sugar water, but they can bring hummingbirds into easy view from lawn chairs, a patio, or a window. If properly mixed, the solution will be very close in strength and sugar content to the nectar the birds obtain from flowers. So long as the small insects and spiders hummingbirds feed upon

Hummingbirds are frequent visitors to yards and gardens. Their fearlessness makes them at home even in the presence of people.

Hummingbird Flower Structure (Fuchsia Cutaway)

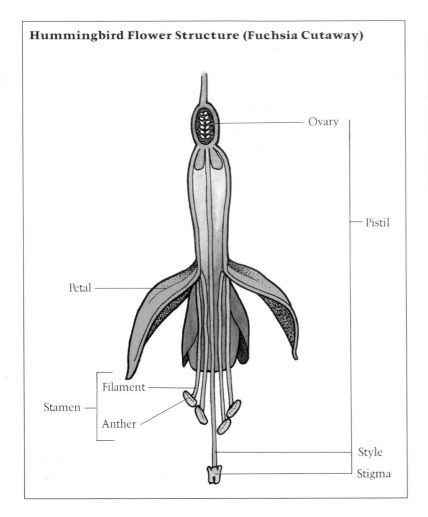

are present in the vicinity, the feeder will take care of their other dietary needs.

For many people there is ample satisfaction in attracting only a few hummingbirds. This is easy to do with a few flowers and a feeder or two. You could set up a small-scale program on a balcony or patio with a feeder and flowers in window boxes, pots, and tubs. Soon you may recognize each hummingbird by its plumage and behavior, and individual birds might become tame enough to land on your finger or shoulder. There have even been cases of hummingbirds recognizing the person who feeds them and following this person about the yard.

One word of warning about a hummingbird-attracting program: It is not fair to hummingbirds to win them over and then suddenly terminate your favors. If for some reason you leave during a critical time of the year, make provision for someone else to look after the flowers and see to the feeders. Once a program has been started, it should continue year after year. When hummingbirds return in the spring, they look for the flowers and feeders they visited the year before, searching in exactly the same places. Although hummingbirds are capable of adjusting to change, they come to rely upon a dependable source of food.

NECTAR FLOWERS

Nectar is the sweet secretion that flowers produce to attract insects or birds that will serve as pollinators. By distributing pollen to other flowers of the same kind, the insect or bird is rewarded and the plant is fertilized. Hummingbirds are among the most important bird pollinators in North America.

However, even the best hummingbird flowers do not always produce a good flow of nectar. The production of nectar slows or stops when the weather is too hot or cold, too wet or dry, or if the wind is very strong. Added to these uncertainties are competitors for the food source that either rob the nectar by slitting the base of the blossom or remove it in the same way that hummingbirds do. To make sure that there is an adequate amount of nectar for all users, gardeners should have a variety of

flowers and sizable numbers of the best ones. This is not to say, however, that a very small garden or flowers in baskets, planters, and window boxes do not offer suitable supplies of nectar. They do, but on a smaller scale.

A well-rounded garden will contain flowers for both hummingbirds and butterflies. If for no other purpose than diverting bees from competing at hummingbird plants, there should be flowers specifically attractive to bees as well if space permits. Finally, the gardener should not exclude plants that are old favorites or which add to the color scheme. Many times these plants are useful as well as decorative. Hummingbirds may visit them for insects, use them as perches, and, if trees or shrubs, build their nests in them. There are few plants that do not in some way fit into a garden designed for hummingbirds and butterflies.

Hummingbird Flowers

In a special group of their own are nectar flowers that have become adapted to pollination by hummingbirds during the course of their evolu-

tion (see Nectar From Plants, page 16). These flowers are tubular, rich in nectar, lacking in fragrance, and structurally designed to be accessible to hummingbirds and inaccessible to other nectar feeders.

Typical hummingbird plants produce multiple flowers in open inflorescences. The flowers are on the outside of the plant, positioned where hummingbirds can feed from them without hitting their wings against the foliage. In some hummingbird plants the flowers are pendant, their openings accessible only to a bird or insect that can hover below and turn its head upward to feed.

The hummingbird flower is usually red, but it may also be orange-red, orange, or pink. Butterfly flowers share some of the characteristics of hummingbird flowers: They are also tubular and rich in nectar, but they are usually fragrant and offer perches or platforms where the butterfly can settle when feeding. There is some overlap in color: Butterfly flowers are red, purple, lavender, yellow, orange, or white and sometimes red. Bees, in contrast, are

Left: Flowers should be easily accessible to hummingbirds, who often take nectar while hovering. Shown here is a Costa's Hummingbird.
Right: Unlike hummingbirds, butterflies frequently choose fragrant flowers that offer platforms where they can perch while taking nectar. Here is a Silver-spotted Skipper on a zinnia.

generally attracted to flowers that are blue, yellow, violet, or in the ultraviolet range.

The fact that nectar feeders are primarily drawn to flowers that suit their feeding methods and that they can tell them by their color reduces competition and saves them energy. It is especially important that hummingbirds, with their limited energy resources, not be compelled to visit every flower they see. However, once hummingbirds spend an appreciable amount of time at any one place, they learn which flowers offer them nectar and visit them regardless of color.

During migration, flower color becomes even more important. On stops between long flights, hummingbirds must be able to recognize good nectar flowers immediately without having to search for them. Red offers them a reliable clue. It is significant that along mountain migration routes, there is no shortage of red wildflowers during spring and late summer.

There are many cultivated varieties of hummingbird flowers that have a place in the garden or window box. Their bright colors offer one of the best advertisements we can offer to both resident and migrant hummingbirds. A whole bed of scarlet sage, for example, can hardly escape notice. And the flowers not only attract hummingbirds but add beauty and color to the garden. They are easy to grow and readily obtainable at most nurseries and garden shops.

Among the native hummingbird plants found in North America are a number that fit well into any garden and others that are essentially wildflowers. The list includes impatiens (*Impatiens*), trumpet creeper (*Campsis radicans*), cardinal flower (*Lobelia cardinalis*), orange honeysuckle (*Lonicera ciliosa*), ocotillo (*Fouquieria splendens*), red buckeye (*Aesculus pavia*), beebalm (*Monarda didyma*), sage (*Salvia*), California fuchsia (*Zauschneria californica*), gilia (*Gilia*), columbine

Left: Hummingbirds are drawn to the brilliant red of a bed of scarlet sage. Red flowers are highly visible against a green background and less likely to draw bees, who do not see colors at the red end of the spectrum.
Right: Ocotillo, a wildflower, is a favored hummingbird plant in the southwestern United States.

(*Aquilegia*), scarlet larkspur (*Delphinium cardinale*), bouvardia (*Bouvardia*), paintbrush (*Castilleja*), red-flowering currant (*Ribes sanguineum*), crimson monkeyflower (*Mimulus cardinalis*), penstemon (*Penstemon*), figwort (*Scrophularia coccinea*), and century plant (*Agave americana*). A number of plant families are represented in hummingbird flowers, especially the mints (*Labiatae*), buttercups (*Ranunculaceae*), and figworts (*Scrophulariaceae*). See also the chart of hummingbird flowers on pages 48 to 51 and the favorite plants mentioned in the hummingbird gallery beginning on page 89.

Among the flowers introduced from South America that have special hummingbird appeal are fuchsia (*Fuchsia*), begonia (*Begonia*), canna (*Canna*), certain species of abutilons (*Abutilon*) and erythrinas (*Erythrinas*), lantana (*Lantana*), also a good butterfly plant, and tree tobacco (*Nicotiana glauca*). Although not all of these plants have specially adapted hummingbird flowers, all are easily recognized by hummingbirds and freely visited by them.

A number of other flowers attractive to hummingbirds have been introduced to the warmer regions of North America. Australia has furnished the eucalyptus (*Eucalyptus*), bottlebrushes (*Callistemon*), powder-puffs (*Calliandra*), and silk-oaks (*Grevillea robusta*). Asia has provided hibiscus (*Hibiscus*), silk tree (*Albizia julibrissin*), and weigela (*Weigela*). Cape-honeysuckle (*Tecomaria capensis*) and red-hot-poker (*Kniphofia uvaria*) are among Africa's contributions.

CHOOSING THE RIGHT FLOWERS

With such a wide selection of flowers to choose from, it is often hard to know which ones to plant. Hummingbird appeal is only one consideration. You should also consider whether the plant is well suited to your locality and whether it is available locally. One of the best ways to find answers to these questions is to look around and see what your neighbors are growing. Choose a time during the blooming season when hummingbirds are about.

Eucalyptus trees offer both nectar and shelter for hummingbirds.

The fact that a flower is being visited by a hummingbird does not necessarily mean that it is well suited for planting in a hummingbird garden. Hummingbirds visit flowers of all kinds in their quest for nectar and small insects. A good hummingbird plant will be visited regularly and for a long enough time for the hummingbird to sample its nectar. Once you've identified the plants hummingbirds prefer, check whether they are fairly common in your area. If they are grown in any number, they are obviously well adapted to local conditions. Inquire at nurseries and garden centers to confirm your conclusions.

Finally, you will need to address such important questions as whether the plant is an annual or perennial, what the blooming season is, whether it requires a sunny or shady location, what its soil requirements are, and whether it suits your hardiness zone. You will need to ask the same questions about plants that may not be growing locally but which are known to be good hummingbird plants. Looking around and experimenting are keys to having a successful

hummingbird garden. The chart on pages 48 to 51 provides a place to start. It gives information on a number of good plants for hummingbird gardens in North America.

Blossoms Throughout the Season

The most challenging part in planning a hummingbird garden is finding plants that will provide blossoms throughout the season when hummingbirds are present. There should be little trouble finding plants for late spring and early summer; this is a peak blooming season for many flowers. Not so easy is finding plants that will bloom during the dry season of late summer or, hardest of all, during winter and early spring in the warm parts of North America. In cold-winter regions, there will be no hummingbirds aside from the occasional stray that may not have been able to find its way south.

Planting some flowers with long blooming seasons and others with shorter ones to fill in when nectar demand is greatest is the most practical and effective approach. Continual flowering is not difficult to achieve with a

A good hummingbird plant is one visited frequently and for relatively long periods. Shown here is a female Calliope Hummingbird determining nectar availability.

selection of annuals, perennials, and a few vines, shrubs, and trees.

Annuals

Because of their long blooming seasons and showy flowers, annuals are extremely popular. They take somewhat more work in planting and preparing soil than other plants, but most gardeners feel that they are well worth the effort. Annuals provide color when few other plants are in bloom. They are commonly used as border plants and to fill beds and window boxes. Start annuals from seeds or purchase plants from garden centers.

Annuals that have long blooming seasons and reasonably strong hummingbird appeal include annual larkspur (*Consolida*), annual phlox (*Phlox drummondii*), garden balsam (*Impatiens balsamina*), nasturtium (*Tropaeolum majus*), petunia (*Petunia*), scarlet sage (*Salvia splendens*), spiderflower (*Cleome spinosa*), and zinnia (*Zinnia*). Scarlet runner bean (*Phaseolus coccineus*) and lupine (*Lupinus*) have relatively short blooming seasons but are good hummingbird plants. Scarlet runner bean blooms from mid- until late summer; lupine has a peak blooming season in June. Interestingly, marigold (*Tagetes*), one of the most commonly planted annuals, has no hummingbird appeal.

Perennials

Herbaceous plants that have a garden life of at least three years, perennials are easier to grow than annuals, because you need not put in new plants every year. Although many die down in

Left: Coralbells, a late-spring bloomer, are a particularly attractive hummingbird perennial.
Right: Petunias have a long blooming season and can provide nectar during periods when other plants are less likely to be in bloom.

winter, they come up again in spring. Where temperatures reach below freezing, some must spend the winter indoors. Perennials are most commonly used as border plants and are planted in the open where there is full sun. Like annuals, they are frequently purchased as growing plants from garden centers. Color, height, and soil preferences should be taken into consideration when choosing perennials.

Two groups of western wildflowers that attract hummingbirds—the paintbrushes (*Castilleja*) and monkeyflowers (*Mimulus*) — include perennials with very long blooming seasons. But most perennials limit their flowering seasons to shorter periods of the year. Columbine (*Aquilegia*) comes into bloom in early spring and continues to blossom into early summer. Late spring and early summer bloomers among the perennials include canna (*Canna*), coralbells (*Heuchera sanguinea*), delphinium (*Delphinium*), gladiolus (*Gladiolus*), iris (*Iris*), lousewort (*Pedicularis canadensis*), and red-hot-poker (*Kniphofia uvaria*). Blooming mid- to late summer are such perennials as

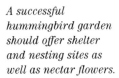

A successful hummingbird garden should offer shelter and nesting sites as well as nectar flowers.

cardinal flower (*Lobelia cardinalis*), beebalm (*Monarda didyma*), and hollyhock (*Alcea*).

Woody Vines, Shrubs, and Trees

The ideal hummingbird garden includes areas of dense shade, partial shade, and open sun. Vines, shrubs, and trees provide these different spaces and also serve as nesting sites for the hummingbirds. Frequently the nest is saddled to a limb or placed in a groove made by two forking branches. Woody plant fibers and soft, fluffy down from the undersides of leaves are important sources of nesting material. This is also true of the lichens on bark, which hummingbirds use as camouflage on the outsides of their nests. However, vines, shrubs, and trees need not be present in your own yard; they serve just as well in neighboring yards or nearby streets.

Some of the very best nectar sources for hummingbirds are the blossoms of woody plants. Like perennials, a number of species offer nectar at seasons when hummingbirds most need it. In California, where the Allen's,

Anna's, and Costa's hummingbirds overwinter, eucalyptus trees (*Eucalyptus*) supply a vital source of nectar. Red-flowering gum (*Eucalyptus ficifolia*) blooms all year, and the swamp mahogany (*Eucalyptus robusta*) and several other species bloom in winter. Orange trees (*Citrus sinensis*) are also winter bloomers. Their nectar-rich flowers are an important source of food for hummingbirds that overwinter in Florida, southern Texas, and southern California.

Powder-puffs (*Calliandra haematocephala*), silk-oaks (*Grevillea robusta*), cape-honeysuckle (*Tecomaria capensis*), and tree tobacco (*Nicotiana glauca*) bloom throughout most of the year in the southern part of the United States. Farther north, winter jasmine (*Jasminum nudiflorum*), winter-blooming camellia (*Camellia*), and the early blossoms of red-flowering currant (*Ribes sanguineum*), flowering quince (*Chaenomeles*), fuchsia (*Fuchsia*), and orange honeysuckle (*Lonicera ciliosa*) provide nectar at times when hummingbirds most need it.

Top: The nectar-rich flowers of eucalyptus trees are an important source of food for hummingbirds. Zauschneria, often called hummingbird-flower, is a favorite of western hummingbirds. Bottom: Plants attractive to hummingbirds can also be an important design element in any garden. Here, Justicia spicigera *lines a walkway and shades a window.*

During late summer, when few flowers are likely to be in bloom for the hummingbirds that will soon depart southward, there are the orange-red blossoms of trumpet creeper (*Campsis radicans*), the fuzzy pink blossoms of silk tree (*Albizia julibrissin*), and the honey-scented ones of common butterfly bush (*Buddleia davidii*). Although butterfly bush is an outstanding butterfly plant, its flowers are also a favorite of hummingbirds and sphinx moths.

DESIGNING A HUMMINGBIRD GARDEN

Establishing a hummingbird garden is much the same as establishing any other garden. Trees and shrubs are generally planted in the fall and bedding plants put in during the spring after the danger of frost has passed. Design considerations are also similar. Smaller plants, primarily annuals, are often used to line walkways and flower beds, with perennials and other taller plants behind them. Apply the

Sage is available in a variety of colors that when grouped together attract hummingbirds and please the eye.

same pattern to trees and shrubs—smaller plants in front and progressively taller ones behind. Although shrubs have an important place as hedge plants and as foundation plantings around the house, shrubs in a hummingbird garden ideally are in the open, where hummingbirds can easily reach the blossoms.

Trees are useful in providing shade and are also valuable as nesting sites and sources of nesting material. Evergreen trees make effective windbreaks and provide shelter to birds and other wildlife. Hummingbirds nest in both evergreen and deciduous plants.

The hummingbird garden should not be cluttered with large trees and shrubs. As you design the garden, leave enough open space for hummingbirds to conduct their aerial displays and move freely from one nectar source to another. A good balance is about one fourth of the yard shaded, one fourth partially shaded, and the rest sufficiently open for the sun to get through during most of the day. In terms of plantings this means that about half the yard

Hummingbird Garden—Plan View

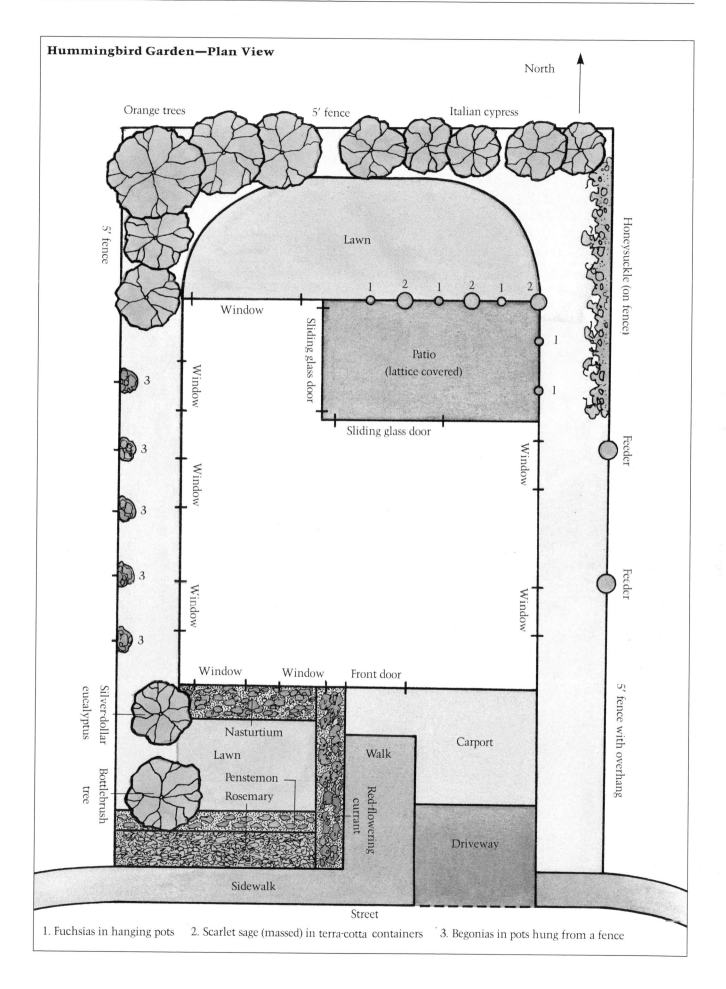

North

Orange trees   5' fence   Italian cypress

5' fence

5' fence

Honeysuckle (on fence)

Lawn

Window

Window

Window

Window

3

3

3

3

Patio
(lattice covered)

Sliding glass door

Sliding glass door

Window

Window

1

1

Feeder

Feeder

5' fence with overhang

Silver-dollar eucalyptus

Bottlebrush tree

Window   Window   Front door

Nasturtium

Lawn

Penstemon

Rosemary

Walk

Red-flowering currant

Carport

Driveway

Sidewalk

Street

1. Fuchsias in hanging pots   2. Scarlet sage (massed) in terra-cotta containers   3. Begonias in pots hung from a fence

should be devoted to lawn or ground cover or flower beds.

Curving flower beds and clusters of trees and shrubs are generally more pleasing to the eye than plants in straight lines. These informal arrangements also better suit the needs of hummingbirds because they can approach the blooms from several sides.

Provide adequate space around plantings for hummingbirds to maneuver into position. This is not to say that every plant in a hummingbird garden should be separated from its neighbors. A bed of brightly colored flowers planted close together is as good an advertisement to hummingbirds as any. Scarlet sage (*Salvia splendens*) is an excellent plant to use for this purpose. Its flowers are on the outside of the plant where hummingbirds can easily reach them, and the brilliant red of a bed of scarlet sage is so colorful that hummingbirds will surely notice the yard from a distance and begin visiting it for nectar.

Considerations such as these make a difference. With a little planning a garden can have both attractive plantings and hummingbirds year after year.

This garden was designed for optimum appeal to hummingbirds. Flowers offer nectar; shrubs and trees provide shelter. The different blooming cycles of the various flowers ensure that nectar will be available over a long period.

Shelter and a Place to Perch

Although hummingbirds may appear to be active every minute of the day, this is far from true. They follow periods of activity with longer periods of almost complete inactivity. During the course of a day, hummingbirds divide their time between visiting flowers for nectar, chasing insects, and perching quietly. They spend approximately four fifths of each day perched in trees or bushes near nectar and other food sources. At roughly regular intervals of from 10 to 15 minutes, the birds leave their perch to feed.

Although males will perch almost anywhere in the open—on exposed twigs, clotheslines, TV antennae, and overhead wires—females and immature birds are more likely to remain hidden somewhere within a tree, shrub, or vine. At night, hummingbirds, regardless of their sex or age, roost in dense cover. Females incubating eggs or brooding young stay on the nests they have built. These are almost always in sheltered places. Non-nesting birds spend the night perched well within the protective shelter of dense foliage. Here, sheltered from the weather, they remain until early dawn.

Plants already in the garden are often well suited for perching places and shelter. Hummingbirds will also perch on some of the plants that they visit for nectar. In the Deep South, citrus trees (*Citrus*), cape-honeysuckle (*Tecomaria capensis*), bottlebrush (*Callistemon*), and bougainvillea (*Bougainvillea*) provide both food and cover. In southern and middle latitudes, the same services are provided by silk tree (*Albizia julibrissin*), weigela (*Weigela*), and beauty bush (*Kolkwitzia amabilis*). Large trees in the yard also provide shelter. Hummingbirds often roost and seek cover in oaks, sycamores, maples, and conifers.

Container Plants

Plants in containers provide excellent nectar sources in early spring before garden plants are in bloom. Keep the containers indoors during cold weather, and on warm days place them in open areas where hummingbirds will find them. The first warm days of spring are when most hummingbirds begin making an appearance. The flowers that you put out may be among the first that they see. Use feeders as a supplemental food source until enough garden plants are in bloom to provide sufficient nectar during the critical period of early spring.

In a limited space—a patio, deck, or veranda plants in baskets, pots, window boxes, planters, and other containers offer a way to attract hummingbirds and provide them places to stay and nest. In larger gardens, container plantings provide variety and can be a strong design element.

Fuchsias are a favorite hummingbird plant and are well suited to growing in containers. Their red tubular or bell-shaped flowers are typical sources of nectar for hummingbirds. Although they do best in a moist, cool climate, such as that of the Pacific Northwest, they can be grown almost anywhere so long as they are planted in good soil, given sufficient shade, and are kept well watered. One of the most effective cool-climate fuchsias for attracting hummingbirds is Magellan fuchsia (*Fuchsia magellanica*). There are many other useful varieties of fuchsia—consult a garden center for one that is suited to your area.

Other plants commonly used in hanging baskets in hummingbird gardens include annual phlox (*Phlox drummondii*), basket begonia

Hummingbirds are fearless creatures and are drawn to wherever nectar is available in some abundance. Small urban gardens, decks, and balconies provide ample space to attract hummingbirds.

Monkeyflowers, a western wildflower, are favored by hummingbirds because of their rich nectar production.

(*Begonia*), nasturtium (*Tropaeolum majus*), petunia (*Petunia*), and snapweed (*Impatiens wallerana*). Although all of these flowers attract hummingbirds to some degree, the two best ones are nasturtium and snapweed. Snapweeds with red blossoms are particularly favored.

Window boxes are just as versatile as hanging baskets, and most of the plants used in hanging baskets are equally well suited to window boxes. Scarlet sage (*Salvia splendens*), known for its hummingbird appeal, does well in window boxes. Coral-fountain (*Russelia*) is a tropical species suited for pots, window boxes, and hanging baskets. For a tropical plant almost sure to capture the attention of the first hummingbirds in spring, there is nothing like Chinese hibiscus (*Hibiscus rosa-sinensis*) with its bright red blossoms.

For those with very limited space, a few pots on the steps and a hanging basket or window box somewhere will always suffice. The hummingbird's fearlessness, which is such a deeply ingrained trait, assures us that they will come to flowers no matter how close we place them to human activities.

Wildflowers

Wildflowers generally offer more nectar than the cultivars that have been derived from them, and wildflowers, of course, are an excellent choice for natural settings. In the West, paintbrushes (*Castilleja*) and monkeyflowers (*Mimulus*)—both stunning wildflowers that are also outstanding hummingbird plants—will grow well with little attention in many gardens. In the southwestern United States many residents position century plants (*Agave americana*) or ocotillos (*Fouquieria splendens*) to accent the lines of their ranch-style homes. Both are among the most highly rated of the desert hummingbird plants.

For those who live in more eastern parts of North America, there are equally good hummingbird plants for the wilder portions of one's property. Jewelweed (*Impatiens capensis*) grows in acid soil in wet woodland. Cardinal flower (*Lobelia cardinalis*) is found in similar habitat and often grows at the edge of fresh water. American columbine (*Aquilegia canadensis*) prefers alkaline soil in more open situations where rocks are present. All three of these wildflowers are attractive and supply hummingbirds with nectar over a long period of time—the columbine in early spring and the jewelweed and cardinal flower in summer.

Water

The daily liquid intake of hummingbirds is as much as eight times their body weight. Much of this is in the form of nectar and sap from trees, but, like other birds, they drink water from whatever sources are available. If they can, they will avoid coming to the ground to drink or bathe. Often they will bathe by flying through fine spray from a waterfall or, in the garden, from a sprinkler system or hand-held hose.

Water in a birdbath is normally much too deep for hummingbirds. But if it is very shallow, they will bathe in it in much the same way as other birds, ducking the head under and using the bill to flip water over the back. They will also dip down to water while in flight, barely touching the surface with their breast feathers. After a wetting, a hummingbird will go to a perch to shake off the water and preen its feathers.

Water is one of the few essential hummingbird needs not produced by plants. Yet many plants do collect raindrops or dew on their leaves, and hummingbirds will use it for drinking and bathing. In fact, if there is any source of water available hummingbirds will find ways to use it. A well-watered garden makes a much better hummingbird habitat than one that is dry.

In the Southwest, century plant is used by both gardeners and hummingbirds.

Red is often used to help hummingbirds identify feeders. All feeder parts, including decorative openings, must be kept scrupulously clean. Shown here is a male Anna's Hummingbird.

USING HUMMINGBIRD FEEDERS

For most hummingbird gardeners, feeders offer a new hobby and a new challenge. Often gardeners find that they enjoy the many small chores that are a part of the daily routine of feeding hummingbirds. Best of all is seeing hummingbirds close by as they come to the feeders to drink. From a nearby vantage point, their glittering plumage can be seen under different light conditions and their antics watched at leisure.

There is also a feeling of satisfaction in knowing that adequate food is always available for them. Flowers may not always provide a lot of nectar and, if there are many hummingbirds, there may be insufficient flowers to meet their demands. The challenge is to supply syrup at the feeders for as long as hummingbirds are present.

Choosing a Feeder

Begin a hummingbird feeding program on a small scale. It can take months for hummingbirds to notice a feeder and begin feeding from it. If they have been in the habit of visiting flowers in a garden, they will likely discover a feeder that has been well placed and contains enough red on it to attract their attention.

Begin by offering hummingbirds sugar water in simple homemade feeders or the type of pet store water bottles used for guinea pigs, hamsters, and cage birds. Most consist of inverted glass bottles with a glass tube at the bottom through which pets can drink. The liquid is held in place by a vacuum created at the top of the bottle. Most hummingbird feeders are of this design.

Simple homemade feeders can be made from a glass test tube, plastic pill jar, or glass jar hung at an angle and filled with sugar water. So long as there is an opening at the upper end through which the hummingbird can insert its bill, these small improvised feeders will demonstrate whether hummingbirds are present in the area and whether they are likely to use feeders. They will also help you find the best locations to place more permanent feeders. Like the store-bought feeders, the homemade ones should display some red on them to advertise their presence to hummingbirds. Red fingernail polish around the opening, a red ribbon attached to the container, or some other red marking should be sufficient.

Once you have determined that hummingbirds are coming regularly to the yard and are visiting both flowers and the improvised feeders, install higher-quality commercial feeders. Insist on a feeder that is durable, easy-to-clean, easy-to-fill, and easy for hummingbirds to feed from. Most popular brands meet these requirements. It is wiser to buy a relatively expensive feeder than to buy one that will fall apart in a year or so, or be difficult for hummingbirds to feed from.

Begin with small models that hold half a pint of liquid (8 ounces) and accommodate as many as three hummingbirds at a time. Several feeders of this size will suffice if there are no more than a dozen hummingbirds in the yard. If the population grows and, as is often the case, more and more appear during migration periods, consider introducing larger feeders. With models that hold as much as a quart of liquid and accommodate as many as eight hummingbirds at a time, it is not necessary to fill the feeders as often.

In hot weather, vacuum-type feeders tend to drip as the air at the top of the reservoir expands, forcing liquid out the openings where hummingbirds feed. This is a problem both because of the waste of liquid and because the fallen liquid attracts ants and other insects. Place feeders in the shade to avoid this problem. In feeders that have openings above the reservoir, drip is not a problem.

Finding a hummingbird feeder that meets all these many requirements may be a little difficult. The best to hope for is an unbreakable and easy-to-clean one that will meet most of our expectations. Hummingbirds, on their part, are easy to please and always hungry. They will feed from any feeder that allows them space for maneuvering and suitable openings into which to thrust their bills.

Placing Feeders

At first feeders need to be placed where birds are most likely to see them—near flowers and in the sun. Later, after one or more hummingbirds are in the habit of visiting the feeders, it will be necessary to move them to other more permanent locations. As you decide where to hang your feeders, for the long term, consider such factors as distance from the house, proximity to cover, importance of shade, and reducing competition among the birds.

Distance from the house Feeders should be readily visible from windows or other vantage points both so that you can see the hummingbirds as they come to feed and so that you can monitor the feeders themselves. The hummingbirds' safety is a primary concern in the placement of feeders; the birds can easily injure themselves by flying into windows or wire screens. If hummingbirds are unfamiliar with windows, they may mistake them for an opening or become confused by reflections in the glass. Hummingbirds will sometimes see red objects inside the house and try to reach them.

Place feeders close to windows so that they become familiar with the glass and come to recognize it as a barrier. A number of feeder models are equipped with suction cups so that you can attach them directly to a windowpane.

Feeder placement is crucial to the success of a hummingbird feeding program. A number of different locations may have to be tried before one suitable to both hummingbird visitors and human spectators is found.

away than 15 feet, hummingbirds will be reluctant to visit them.

Importance of shade   The problem of feeder solution dripping from warm feeders (page 43) will be much less of a nuisance if feeders are kept in the shade. In addition, if the feeder is not exposed to direct sunlight, the solution will spoil less rapidly. However, for those who wish to see a hummingbird in full glory as the sun brings out its color, shade is a drawback. A reasonable compromise is to place feeders where they will be in the shade most of the day yet in the sun for at least a few hours. In cool weather there is no harm in placing feeders in the sun.

Reducing competition   Hummingbirds always engage in a certain amount of chasing and challenging each other whether they feed at flowers or sugar-water feeders. This is part of their normal behavior and nothing to be concerned about. However, when an unusually aggressive bird (often an adult male) attempts to keep all the others away from the feeders, something may have to be done to reduce the competition. The problem is most worrisome if only a few hummingbirds are visiting the feeders. The aggressive bird may be able to prevent the others from feeding. Watching from a prominent perch, he immediately gives chase as soon as another bird appears. If as many as 10 or more birds are visiting a feeder, the bully may find it impossible to keep them all away. While giving chase to one bird, the others are able to feed at least briefly without being molested.

The best way to cope with aggressive birds is to keep your feeders well apart so that no one bird will be able to dominate all of them. An aggressive bird will attempt to dominate only the feeders that are clearly visible from its perch. Feeders can be placed either on different sides of the house or where vegetation hides one feeder from another. The most effective plan might be to provide the aggressive bird with a feeder of its very own that is at some distance from the other feeders.

Each situation calls for a slightly different arrangement. Be prepared for a feeding problem of this kind by having a number of feeders available so that you can use them in whatever ways seem most appropriate.

Not all feeders need to be this close. Birds coming to more distant feeders—15 or 20 feet away—are less likely to fly into windows. However, feeders placed farther away from the house must still be carefully monitored for cleanliness (see page 45) and solution supply.

Proximity to cover   Feeders should be within 10 or 15 feet of the nearest cover. Hummingbirds spend a large portion of their time perched in a tree or shrub. Here, safe from predators, they wait until it is necessary to fly out in search of food. The closer they are to a food supply, the less energy they will expend and the shorter the distance they need fly if danger looms. If the feeders are much farther

Preparing the Syrup Solution

The standard syrup solution for feeding hummingbirds consists of 1 part white sugar to 4 parts water. Begin by stirring the sugar into the water, then bring the solution to a boil over low heat. Boiling is important as it kills mold spores and bacteria and, through evaporation, reduces any chlorine or fluorine that may be in the water. Hummingbirds are known to avoid solutions that contain chemicals.

Prolonged boiling is unnecessary—two minutes is long enough. Overboiling will remove too much water, making the solution stronger than a 1:4 ratio.

After the solution has been allowed to cool, it is ready to be placed in the feeders. If it is being saved for later use, it should be stored in a refrigerator.

Cleaning Feeders

One of the most important of the small chores connected with feeding hummingbirds is cleaning the feeders. Unless this is done at least every three days in hot weather and every six or seven days in cool weather, the solution becomes cloudy. Careful examination will reveal small black specks in the liquid and mold beginning to form on the inside of the plastic or glass reservoir holding the solution. These are danger signals. Harmful bacteria and mold represent health risks to hummingbirds and could kill them.

Without waiting for the solution to go sour or ferment, you should make it a routine to take down the feeders every few days, empty any leftover solution, and rinse them in warm water before adding fresh solution. If mold has already begun to form, you will need to do much more thorough cleaning. By adding vinegar and grains of uncooked rice to the rinse and shaking the feeder vigorously you can loosen most of the mold. Then empty the feeder and rinse it again using warm water. If some mold still remains, you may need to scrub it off with small percolator brushes or with bottle brushes that have stiff wire handles.

A common complaint among novices is that the birds are ignoring their feeders. Often the reason is that the solution has become sour and, as a result, the birds are not drinking it. When you start a feeding program, pour only a small amount of sugar water into a feeder. In this way, you will waste only a very little when

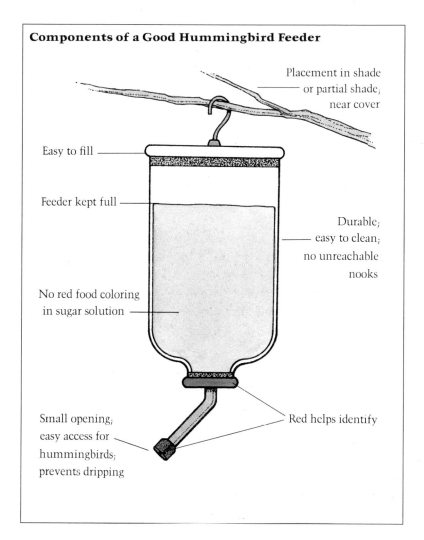

Components of a Good Hummingbird Feeder

Placement in shade or partial shade; near cover

Easy to fill

Feeder kept full

Durable; easy to clean; no unreachable nooks

No red food coloring in sugar solution

Small opening; easy access for hummingbirds; prevents dripping

Red helps identify

the time comes to empty the feeder and add more solution.

Deterring Ants, Bees, and Wasps

Some of the same insects that compete with hummingbirds at flowers are attracted to hummingbird feeders. This is true of bees and wasps but not of sphinx moths or butterflies, which almost never visit feeders. Bees, wasps, and close relatives among the Hymenoptera visit the feeders for the same reason that hummingbirds do—for the sweet-tasting solution. If overly numerous they keep hummingbirds away and drain the feeders. They are a nuisance to gardeners as well.

There are a number of ways to discourage these insect pests. One is to use bee guards—small screens that come with many commercial feeders and fit over the feeding ports. Bees and their relatives are unable to reach the solution through the guards, but it is still accessible to hummingbirds with their long, slender bills. The guards must be cleaned frequently as the hummingbirds splatter them with sugar water as they feed, which attracts insects. Also the hummingbirds are somewhat inconvenienced by the guards.

A second way of dealing with the insect pests is to smear the surfaces around the feeding openings with slippery substances that will prevent the insects from getting a foothold. Petroleum jelly, salad oil, or mineral oil can be used for this purpose. Apply only a little and be sure not to let any get in the feeder and contaminate the solution. If the insects persist in coming back, you will need to smear the surfaces again from time to time.

Avoid using pesticides to combat the pests. Both the hummingbirds and the small insects they need for food could be adversely affected.

As long as a plentiful supply of natural nectar is available for bees and their close relatives, they are unlikely to visit hummingbird feeders. Late fall, when few flowers are in bloom, is the season to expect bees. But by then, except in the warm southern regions, hummingbird feeding is over for the year.

Ants are also attracted to sweet solutions but are less of a problem than bees or wasps since there are simple ways of blocking their approach routes. One is to smear the same greasy substances used in combating bees onto the feeder supports. Another method of stopping ants is to block their approach with a water barrier. Many commercial feeders have a small moat around the hanger to which the feeder is attached. Or make your own using a container and wire. There are always ways to solve insect problems at hummingbird feeders—some problems take patience and ingenuity, others are easy to solve. Sometimes all one has to do is move the feeder and hope that the insects do not find it at its new location. Other times, it may be a matter of simply waiting and the problem will solve itself. Other food sources may be close by and the troublesome insects will leave to go to them.

Controlling Other Visitors

Drawn by a universal taste for sweets, a long list of other visitors besides hummingbirds come to sugar-water feeders—lizards, bats, opossums, raccoons, foxes, squirrels, chipmunks, and most families of songbirds. Orioles, accustomed to visiting flowers for nectar, are among the most persistent of the bird visitors,

followed by house finches, warblers, chickadees, and many others. The total number of bird species so far reported at sugar-water feeders has reached 60.

Part of the reason for this variety of visitors is that many people, fascinated by having so many forms of animal life in their yards, have gone out of their way to encourage species other than hummingbirds. Some offer sugar water in open-mouthed jars and place their feeders where other visitors can easily find them. Night-prowling mammals are given feeders on shelves or on the ground. Orioles, among the most popular of the bird visitors, are provided with especially designed feeders that are sold commercially. These are easier for them to

Avoiding Feeding Risks

From time to time mixtures other than sugar water have been proposed for feeding hummingbirds. All of them present unacceptable risks. This is especially true of honey-water mixtures. Not only is honey an unnatural food for hummingbirds, but it spoils much more quickly than sugar water and contains a bacteria that causes a fungus disease on the tongue. The disease is always fatal.

White sugar, on the other hand, is a sucrose sugar like the sucrose in flower nectar. The strength of 1 part sugar to 4 parts water closely approximates the strength of flower nectar. Stronger concentrations have been found to adversely affect the liver of captive birds; weaker concentrations are less attractive to the hummingbirds.

Other mixtures that are unsafe and that should be avoided are those made with artificial sweeteners and those that contain nutritional additives. Hummingbirds supplement their nectar diet with foods they find in the wild, therefore protein supplements are unnecessary; they are also potentially harmful.

The same is true of red food coloring. An artificial dye, red food coloring is often added to mixtures so that hummingbirds, with their well-known affinity for red, will quickly be attracted to the feeder. The safety of red dye has been questioned in regard to its use in foods for human consumption. Nearly all commercial feeders already are decorated with red plastic flowers or tinted with red. Therefore, the addition of red food coloring is unnecessary as well as potentially harmful. Once hummingbirds discover a feeder, they continue coming to it regardless of its color.

Hummingbirds, such as this female Allen's taking nectar from red-hot-poker, provide another dimension of beauty and movement in the garden.

feed from than hummingbird feeders and are even tinted orange, a color that appeals to orioles.

Too much of a good thing, however, can prove to be a nuisance. Some people complain that other birds keep hummingbirds from feeding and use up more than their share of the syrup. In clumsy attempts to reach feeding ports, some birds rock the feeders, causing the solution to spill. Orioles have been observed removing bee guards. Complaints, such as these, can be dealt with by providing alternative feeding places and feeders for the troublemakers. Orioles, for example, find it much

easier to perch while feeding and therefore go to feeders designed for them rather than expend excess energy trying to hover before hummingbird feeders. Similar tactics can be used successfully with the other intruders.

A garden designed for hummingbirds is a special and rewarding place. The presence of hummingbirds adds a unique dimension to an urban or suburban setting. In providing habitat for hummingbirds, gardeners increase their enjoyment and the utility of their yards, and, perhaps most importantly, fulfill the fundamental needs of the gorgeous creatures who will find themselves at home there.

Aloe arborescens (tree aloe)

Aquilegia hybrid (columbine hybrid)

Calliandra haematocephala (pink powder-puff)

Chaenomeles species (flowering quince)

HUMMINGBIRD PLANTS

Botanical and Common Names	Type And Size	Blooming Season	Flower Color(s)	Soil	Light	USDA Zone Adaptation
Abutilon hybridum Abutilon, flowering maple	Evergreen shrub to 8'–10'	Year around	Yellow, red, and white	Well drained, loamy	Full sun	10
Agave americana Century plant	Succulent	Summer	Greenish yellow	Sandy, porous	Full sun	6–10
Albizia julibrissin Silk tree, mimosa	Deciduous tree to 40'	June–August	Pink and white stamens	Sandy or loamy	Full sun	7–10
Aloe species Aloe	Succulents	Varies	Red, orange, yellow, white	Sandy	Full sun	9, 10
Aquilegia canadensis American columbine	Perennial	Early spring–midsummer	Yellow and red	Sandy or rocky, alkaline	Sun or partial shade	2–8
Begonia coccinea Scarlet begonia	Perennial	Almost year around	Coral red	Loamy	Semishade	All, but needs to be indoors in winter
Buddleia davidii Common butterfly bush, summer-lilac	Deciduous or semievergreen shrub to 10'	Late summer–early fall	Lavender, blue, white	Alkaline	Full sun	5–9
Calliandra haematocephala Pink powder-puff	Evergreen shrub to 10'	December–April	Red	Any		10
Callistemon citrinus Lemon bottlebrush	Evergreen shrub or small tree to 10'	Throughout year	Red	Rich, porous	Full sun	9, 10

Fuchsia 'China House' (fuchsia)   *Fuchsia* 'Gartenmeister Bonstedt' (fuchsia)

HUMMINGBIRD PLANTS

Botanical and Common Names	Type And Size	Blooming Season	Flower Color(s)	Soil	Light	USDA Zone Adaptation
Campsis radicans Trumpet creeper, trumpet vine	Deciduous vine	July–September	Orange and red	Well drained, fertile	Full sun	4–9
Castilleja coccinea Scarlet paintbrush, Indian-paintbrush	Perennial	March–October	Scarlet	Loamy, with humus	Full sun	3–9
Chaenomeles species Flowering quince	Deciduous shrubs to 10′	Late winter–early spring	White, pink, orange, red	Loamy	Full sun	4–9
Citrus sinensis Orange	Evergreen tree to 30′	Spring	White	Rich, loamy	Full sun	10
Delphinium cardinale Scarlet larkspur	Perennial	Summer	Scarlet	Rich, somewhat alkaline	Sun or partial shade	8, 9
Eucalyptus species Eucalyptus	Evergreen trees and shrubs, various sizes	Varies	Various, including red	Any	Full sun	9, 10
Fouquieria splendens Ocotillo	Deciduous shrub to 25′	Spring–summer	Scarlet	Well drained	Full sun	9, 10
Fuchsia species Fuchsia	Evergreen or deciduous shrubs	All year around	Pink, red, white, yellow	Rich, moist	Shade	5–10
Grevillea robusta Silk-oak	Evergreen tree to 50′	Spring	Orange	Any	Full sun	10
Grevillea rosmarinifolia Rosemary grevillea	Evergreen shrub to 6′	Nearly year around	Red and cream	Any	Full sun	10

Top: *Kniphofia uvaria* (red-hot-poker)
Bottom: *Salvia* 'Maynight' (sage)

Lupinus densiflorus (lupine)

Top: *Fuchsia* species (fuchsia)
Bottom: *Tropaeolum majus* (nasturtium)

HUMMINGBIRD PLANTS

Botanical and Common Names	Type And Size	Blooming Season	Flower Color(s)	Soil	Light	USDA Zone Adaptation
Heuchera sanguinea Coralbells	Perennial	April–August	Scarlet	Most	Sun or partial shade	5–10
Impatiens capensis Jewelweed	Annual	July–October	Orange-yellow	Moist, acid	Partial shade	2–8
Justicia brandegeana Shrimp-plant	Evergreen shrub to 3'	Year around	White flowers with purple dots	Loamy or sandy, with leaf mold	Light shade	9, 10
Kniphofia uvaria Red-hot-poker	Perennial	Spring–frost	Orange-red	Well drained, sandy or loamy	Full sun	6–10
Lantana camara Lantana	Evergreen shrub to 6'	Year around	Pink, yellow, orange, scarlet	Loamy, with humus	Full sun	8–10
Leonotis leonurus Lion's-tail	Perennial	Fall	Orange-scarlet	Sandy, with humus	Full sun	9, 10
Lobelia cardinalis Cardinal flower	Perennial	July–September	Cardinal red	Rich, moist	Shade	2–7
Lonicera japonica Japanese honeysuckle	Evergreen or deciduous vine	Spring–summer	White, yellow, tinged with purple	Well drained, loamy	Sun or partial shade	3–9
Lonicera sempervirens Trumpet honeysuckle	Evergreen or semievergreen vine	May–August	Orange or scarlet	Well drained, loamy	Sun or partial shade	3–9
Lupinus species Lupine	Annuals and perennials	Spring–summer	White, red, pink, blue	Most	Full sun	4–10
Mimulus aurantiacus Sticky monkeyflower	Perennial	Spring–summer	Orange	Most	Full sun	7–9
Mimulus cardinalis Monkeyflower	Perennial	March–October	Scarlet	Rich, moist	Partial shade	7–9

Tecomaria capensis 'Aurea' (cape-honeysuckle)

Zauschneria californica (California fuchsia, hummingbird-flower)

HUMMINGBIRD PLANTS

Botanical and Common Names	Type And Size	Blooming Season	Flower Color(s)	Soil	Light	USDA Zone Adaptation
Monarda didyma Beebalm	Perennial	June–August	Scarlet	Most	Sun	4–7
Nicotiana glauca Tree tobacco	Evergreen shrub or small tree to 18′	Nearly year around	Greenish yellow	Any	Full sun	9, 10
Pedicularis canadensis Lousewort, woodbetony	Perennial	May–July	Yellow	Any	Sun	3–10
Penstemon cardinalis Beardtongue, scarlet bugler	Perennial	May–July	Red	Well drained, sandy or loamy	Sun or partial shade	9, 10
Petunia × hybrida Petunia	Perennial often used as an annual	Spring–summer	Various	Well drained, light	Full sun	All
Phaseolus coccineus Scarlet runner bean	Climbing annual	Mid- to late summer	Scarlet	Well drained, rich	Full sun	8–10
Rosmarinus officinalis Rosemary	Evergreen shrub to 7′	Autumn and spring	Pink, purple, blue, and violet	Well drained, light	Full sun	6–10
Russelia equisetiformis Coral-fountain	Shrub to 4′	Spring–summer	Red	Loamy	Full sun	9, 10
Salvia splendens Scarlet sage	Perennial or annual	Spring–frost	Scarlet	Fertile	Sun or shade	5–10
Tecomaria capensis Cape-honeysuckle	Evergreen shrub to 8′ or vine to 25′	All year around	Orange-red to scarlet	Fertile	Full sun	9, 10
Trichostema lanatum Woolly bluecurls	Evergreen shrub to 3′–5′	Spring	Purple to blue	Any	Full sun	7, 8
Tropaeolum majus Nasturtium	Perennial or annual	Spring–frost	Yellow, red, orange	Poor, sandy	Sun to partial shade	All
Zauschneria californica California fuchsia, hummingbird-flower	Perennial	Late summer–October	Scarlet	Light, loamy	Full sun	9, 10

Butterflies in the Garden

For centuries, people have been captivated by the exotic nature of butterflies. With an understanding of butterfly needs and careful planning, you can easily make these ethereal creatures a permanent feature of a home landscape—flying flowers that will provide years of pleasure and entertainment.

Adding the beauty and color of butterflies to the garden can be an enjoyable and rewarding experience. Imagine a Tiger Swallowtail butterfly flitting through the garden and landing on a daisy, or a Monarch flying over to a lilac bush for a taste of nectar, or a European Cabbage Butterfly taking nectar from an aster blossom. By planting the specific plants that butterflies like, you can attract these fascinating insects to your garden. Butterflies add color, movement, and beauty to a home garden, and the activities of the many different species are a pleasure to watch.

This chapter provides an introduction to butterflies and the basics of butterfly gardening. It begins with a description of the life cycle of butterflies, from egg to adult, and continues with an overview of butterfly behavior and physical characteristics. Next, you'll learn how to design your garden around the specific needs of butterflies—food sources, sunlight, and shelter. Also included is a chart of 42 of the most popular nectar plants for butterflies, along with information on their appearance and how to grow them.

It is relatively simple to both attract butterflies and have a garden that suits your tastes and needs. Nectar flowers and other favorite

The ideal butterfly garden is full of color and a variety of nectar flowers: black-eyed-susan, yarrow, sedum, and anemone are shown here. Inset: The eyespotted Buckeye butterfly favors areas that combine low vegetation and bare ground.

Top left: This Giant Swallowtail is a member of the swallowtail (Papilionidae) family.
Top right: The often-seen European Cabbage Butterfly is a member of the family Pieridae.
Center right: Members of the family Lycaenidae, such as this Gray Hairstreak, are among the smaller butterflies.
Bottom right: The family Libytheidae (snouts), of which this Eastern Snout butterfly is a member, is the smallest butterfly family.

butterfly plants come in many forms—annuals, perennials, shrubs, vines, and trees—and in colors that range from red to purple to yellow and white.

Whichever plants you choose or wherever you live, you're sure to enjoy a wide assortment of butterfly activities in your garden. You'll perhaps come upon a pair of American Painted Ladies in a courtship flight or a myriad of Clouded Sulfurs in a mud-puddle congregation, a Buckeye basking on a flat stone, or a group of Sleepy Oranges on one of their periodic emigrations, or a Pipe Vine Swallowtail or one of the numerous butterflies that mimic it. Having your own butterfly garden will enable you to witness up close the wonder of butterflies and the flowers on which they feed.

CLASSIFICATION

All butterflies belong to the kingdom Animalia, phylum Arthropoda, class Insecta, and order Lepidoptera. Within the order Lepidoptera there are two superfamilies: true butterflies (Papilionoidea) and skippers (Hesperioidea). Superfamily Papilionoidea comprises five families: swallowtails (Papilionidae) are generally large and have projections like tails from the hind wing; whites and sulfurs (Pieridae) are small or medium sized and are often white or yellow; the gossamer wings (Lycaenidae) consist of mostly small butterflies, such as the blues, hairstreaks, and coppers; the snouts (Libytheidae) consist of butterflies that have extremely long, snoutlike labial palpi (feeding apparatus); and the brush-footed butterflies (Nymphalidae) consist of a wide range of butterflies, including the fritillaries, crescents, satyrs, and milkweed butterflies. Skippers (Hesperiidae) are also grouped with butterflies, but actually belong to a second superfamily—Hesperioidea—of which they are the only member. Skippers are generally small or medium sized and are thick bodied.

DISTRIBUTION

North American butterflies are distributed over many different areas of the continent, from subtropical forests to deciduous woods to alpine summits. Each species chooses a habitat according to the latitude, altitude, availability of host plants, competition with other species,

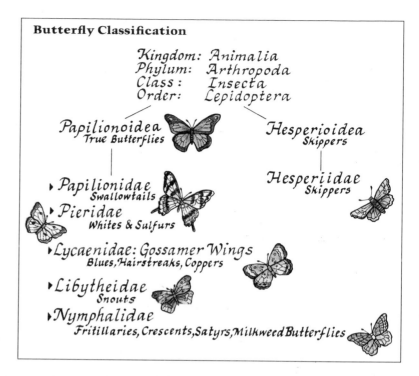

Butterfly Classification

Kingdom: *Animalia*
Phylum: *Arthropoda*
Class: *Insecta*
Order: *Lepidoptera*

Papilionoidea
True Butterflies

▸ *Papilionidae*
Swallowtails
▸ *Pieridae*
Whites & Sulfurs
▸ *Lycaenidae: Gossamer Wings*
Blues, Hairstreaks, Coppers
▸ *Libytheidae*
Snouts
▸ *Nymphalidae*
Fritillaries, Crescents, Satyrs, Milkweed Butterflies

Hesperioidea
Skippers

Hesperiidae
Skippers

The nymphalids are the largest and most varied family of true butterflies. The Monarch is a favorite member.

Skippers, such as this Sachem, belong to the family Hesperiidae.

and other evolutionary factors. For instance, the rare Atala lives in the subtropical scrub found in southeastern Florida, the Diana is adapted to the deciduous forests of the Appalachian mountains, and the Pink-edged Sulfur is a resident of northern evergreen forests.

Many butterfly species, however, have recently extended their range. Throughout North America the changes humans have wrought on the natural environment have created disturbed habitats, places where both native plants and introduced weeds that serve as butterfly host plants have learned to thrive. This has brought about a concurrent spread of many beautiful butterfly species, most of which are ideal for butterfly gardeners, such as the Black Swallowtail, European Cabbage Butterfly, Clouded Sulfur, Orange Sulfur, Cloudless Sulfur, Small (American) Copper, Variegated Fritillary, Great Spangled Fritillary, American Painted Lady, Monarch, Silver-spotted Skipper, Fiery Skipper, and Sachem.

Whether you choose to attract a butterfly that is wide-ranging or one that is common only in your particular area, the principles that apply are the same: Provide the butterfly with what it needs to survive and it will adapt to your garden as it would to other natural and disturbed habitats. For information about the types of butterflies that exist in your area, see the butterfly gallery beginning on page 96.

Top: The Orange Sulfur is one of several species whose range has expanded with the spread of their preferred host plants in urban gardens, pastures, and roadsides.

This American Painted Lady is a striking example of the varied patterns and bright colors that are characteristic of many butterflies.

Butterfly Life Cycle

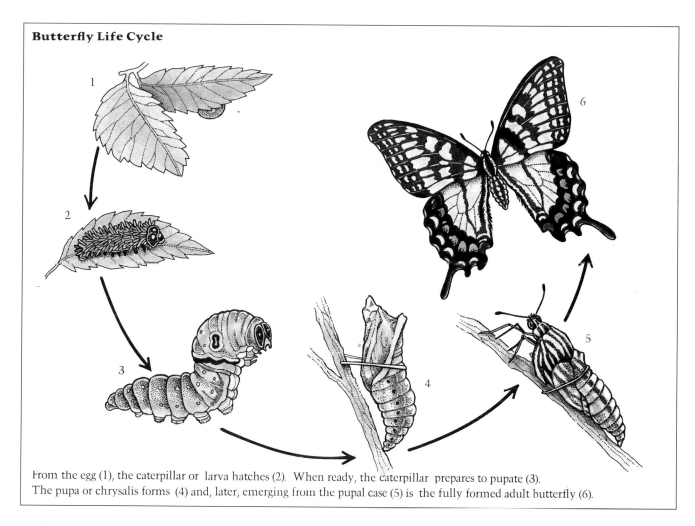

From the egg (1), the caterpillar or larva hatches (2). When ready, the caterpillar prepares to pupate (3). The pupa or chrysalis forms (4) and, later, emerging from the pupal case (5) is the fully formed adult butterfly (6).

FROM EGG TO ADULT

To understand the nature of butterflies and be able to attract them to the garden in the most successful and predictable manner possible, the caring gardener needs a working knowledge of the butterfly's life stages. With this knowledge you can plan your garden to meet the butterflies' food, shelter, and other needs at each stage of the life cycle.

The Beginning of Life

Each butterfly begins life as an egg that is deposited on or near a specific host plant by the female. Eggs come in various shapes, colors, and sizes—oblong, spheroid, ribbed, or smooth—and in shades ranging from yellow and white to green and brown. Some eggs are laid singly, while others are laid in clusters of up to a few hundred. Although eggs are usually deposited on the underside of a host plant leaf, some butterflies (such as the Silver-spotted Skipper) lay their eggs on the plant next to the proper host plant. (After hatching, the tiny caterpillar crawls to the neighboring host plant.)

The Development Continues

Although there are variations among butterfly species, in general eggs complete embryonic development and hatch in 4 to 10 days. When the egg hatches, a tiny caterpillar (or larva) emerges. The larvae of many species eat their eggshells when they first emerge. In other species, the larvae leave the egg and begin eating the host plant with vigor, storing up energy and growing in size. In still other species, the larvae wait until spring to begin eating.

As it grows, the larva sheds its skin a number of times. Like the eggs, larvae come in various shapes, colors, and sizes: Some are dark and spiny, others are green, and still others are cross striped with different colors; some have long, fleshy projections that look like antennae (but are not antennae in the sensory sense); some are large (the Giant Swallowtail is 2⅜ inches), some are medium sized (the Buckeye is 1¼ inches), and some are small (the Common Blue is ⅜ inch).

Most of the time, larvae feed on the underside of the host plant leaves. In general, it is

Left: The whites, such as this Checkered White, are predominantly white with some black marks.
Right: The coloring of the Tiger Swallowtail is a result of pigmentation rather than diffraction.

three or four weeks before a larva is ready to turn into a chrysalis (also called a pupa). However, the larvae of some butterfly species, such as the Great Spangled Fritillary, spend the winter as larvae and even wait until the spring to start eating. In the case of the Silver-spotted Skipper, the first eggs of the season develop directly into butterflies and the second brood spends the winter as larvae. The larvae of some Alpine species take almost two years to develop into adult butterflies.

A Wondrous Transformation

After shedding its skin for the last time, the larva turns into a chrysalis, or pupa. This magical transformation occurs as the larva's skin splits and the larva wriggles so that the wafer-thin skin rolls off its body. Underneath, the pupa is revealed. Pupae come in various shapes, colors, and sizes. Some hang upside down; others rest upright, held in place by a silken girdle that the caterpillar has made before turning into a chrysalis. Some pupae are brown and mottled, some are green, and some are white, orange, and black. But perhaps the most exquisite is that of the Monarch, which is pale green with delicate spots of gold.

It usually takes one or two weeks for the pupa to develop into a butterfly. Some species, such as the swallowtails, however, pass through the winter as pupae. In the spring, usually after the first rains, which nurture the host plants and nectar flowers that the butterflies will be using to survive, these pupae pick up where they left off in the fall and complete their development into adults.

A Beauty Emerges

The adult butterfly emerges from the chrysalis and proceeds out into the world looking for sources of nourishment and a mate with whom to reproduce and start the life cycle all over again. Most butterflies live for 2 or 3 weeks, although some live for as long as 10 months or more, and others live for only a few days. For example, the Spring Azure may live for only 4 days, although the Mourning Cloak (which passes the winter as an adult) may live for as long as 10 or 11 months. The early spring and summer generations of the Monarch may live for a few weeks, although the early fall generation that migrates south will survive for about 6 months before mating and heading back north again.

BUTTERFLY CHARACTERISTICS AND BEHAVIOR

There are large and small butterflies in a range of colors. They have such names as swallowtails and sulfurs, hairstreaks and checkerspots. There is the regal Monarch, the wide-ranging American Painted Lady, and the aptly named skippers—a wealth of butterfly appearances, life habits, and other characteristics to observe.

All butterflies share certain physical features. The head of a butterfly has two large eyes, two antennae, a proboscis through which nectar and other sources of nourishment are ingested, and a pair of labial palpi on either side of the proboscis that house this tubelike organ. All butterflies have six legs, a thorax (midsection), and an abdomen (lower section). See illustration below.

The butterfly's most exquisite feature is its extraordinary wings, which both power it to flight and offer the viewer an astonishing variety of bright colors and patterns. Butterflies have a pair of forewings and a pair of hind wings. Each of these wings has an upper (dorsal) and lower (ventral) surface, along with a series of dark veins that strengthen and pump blood, or hemolymph, through the wings. From the outer (or marginal) area of the wings to the basal area where they join the body is a remarkable series of patterns and colors that distinguish each species of butterfly and many of the butterfly families.

A range of butterfly behavior may be seen in a garden. Butterflies are often looking for nectar, basking in the sun, roosting on the underside of a leaf, or searching for a perch. They display many survival strategies common to all creatures.

On the Wing

Butterflies are cold-blooded, and as such they require the warmth of the sun. Usually butterflies will fly only when the temperature is at least 60° F. The patterns of butterfly flight range from the slow, lilting flight of the Monarch to the erratic darting of a small blue. With practice, you can learn to identify many butterflies as much by their patterns of flight as by other characteristics. Becoming more familiar with habits such as these will bring you closer to the butterflies, and they to you.

A Rainbow of Colors

The many color combinations of butterflies range from the yellow-and-black swallowtails to the tiny blues to the whites and sulfurs, to the orange and black Monarch, and to the richly patterned species such as the eyespotted Buckeye and the American Painted Lady. The color of butterfly wings is formed in one of two ways: Either the scales on the wings have pigment in them, or they refract light the way a prism does, creating structural colors. Some structural colors are iridescent and change depending on the angle at which they are viewed.

Butterfly Anatomy

Forewing

Thorax

Antennae

Head

Labial palpus

Proboscis

Foreleg

Midleg

Hind leg

Hind wing

Abdomen

Top: Butterfly coloration varies seasonally and geographically. Here, the black form of the Tiger Swallowtail is shown.
Bottom: Another example of the range of butterfly colors is this female Spring Azure. This species exhibits a range of seasonal, geographic, and gender-related color variations.

The upper surface of the blues and the lower silver spots of many fritillaries are good examples of structural colors; the blacks, browns, and yellows of other butterflies are good examples of colors that are created by pigments.

Butterfly coloration serves several purposes. It greatly helps males select a mate because they can easily recognize females of the same species by their coloration. There are, however, distinct color variations between the sexes of each species. For example, the males of many blues (the Orange-bordered Blue, for example) are bright blue above and the females of the same species are brownish.

Color also serves to protect butterflies by confusing or distracting predators. The lower surfaces of the wings of some butterflies are cryptic in appearance—that is, they resemble and blend in with the butterfly's natural surroundings—and the upper wing surfaces are boldly patterned. These butterflies avoid predators by first flashing the bright colors of their upper wing surfaces at them while they are in flight. Then when they land, only the cryptic lower surfaces are visible and the butterflies seem to disappear from view.

By learning about the coloration differences between butterflies and the function these colorations serve, you can better understand the behavior and events occurring in the garden. Butterfly colors can also be enjoyed and appreciated for their beauty alone—an orange Gulf Fritillary flying over a blue border of ageratum or a white border of sweet alyssum; a European Cabbage Butterfly flitting around a purple lantana bush; or a Tiger Swallowtail on an orange marigold. The combinations of butterfly and flower colors that can be achieved in the garden are almost endless.

The Courtship Dance

There is perhaps nothing more delicate to watch in the butterfly world than a courting pair of Orange Sulfurs circling upward together into the sky. Regardless of which species visit your garden, you are sure to see some courtship rituals from time to time. The courtship displays of various butterflies provide entertaining moments for the butterfly gardener to observe. The majority of male butterflies use one of two strategies for locating a suitable mate—perching or patrolling. Some males, such as those of the American Painted Lady and the Gray Hairstreak, perch on an open branch and wait for females to pass by; other males, such as those of the Tiger Swallowtail and the Spring Azure, actively patrol an area, searching for receptive females.

Male and female butterflies often do a nuptial "dance" on the ground as the male tries to entice the female to mate; and unreceptive females—including those that have already mated or are of the wrong species—will signal that they are unavailable by spreading their wings and raising their abdomen high into the air, thus making coupling impossible.

Like this pair of European Cabbage Butterflies, butterflies mate by attaching themselves to each other by the tips of their abdomens.

During oviposition, the female curves her abdomen and slowly deposits one or more eggs on the chosen plant.

Butterflies mate by attaching themselves to each other by the tips of their abdomens. Mating can last from a number of minutes to several hours, and sometimes the pair can be seen flying around while coupled. Usually the male carries the female in such cases. In most species, males mate numerous times during their lives. Some females mate only once, while others mate several times.

Laying Eggs

After mating, the female immediately embarks on a search for the proper host plant on which to deposit her eggs. Oviposition—the depositing of eggs by the female on the host plant—usually occurs when the female lands on the host plant and curls her abdomen up onto a leaf, flower bud, or stem. Eggs are laid singly or in clusters, on the underside of the host plant leaf. Some butterflies, such as certain fritillaries, lay their eggs among the vegetation near their favorite host plant (fritillary larvae eat violets). These larvae must find their own way to the host plants.

Test your powers of observation by trying to locate eggs on host plants. Although locating eggs can sometimes be difficult, it is rewarding to find the eggs of your favorite butterflies and

Top: Butterfly eggs generally hatch from within 4 to 10 days. Shown here are Short-tailed Swallowtail eggs. Bottom: This Mourning Cloak is basking on birch leaves, absorbing sufficient warmth for flight and feeding.

witness the beginning of their lives. Follow a female European Cabbage Butterfly on her rounds among cabbage plants and you may find a tiny egg on the underside of a cabbage leaf. Look at the underside of a passion vine leaf for a tiny egg or the black-and-red larva of the Gulf Fritillary, or examine a threadlike fennel leaf for the delicately balanced Anise Swallowtail egg. One of the best indications that there is a larva underneath the leaves of a butterfly host plant is partially eaten leaves or leaves with small holes in them.

Butterfly eggs vary considerably in length, from the relatively large ones of the Monarch, 1.2 mm tall by 0.9 mm wide, to the small eggs of the Long-tailed Skipper, 0.1 mm tall by about 0.1 mm wide.

Basking

Because butterflies are cold-blooded, they need to bask in the sun to absorb enough warmth for flight and other activities. Some butterflies, such as the Monarch and the American Painted Lady, bask with their wings open and perpendicular to the sun's rays; others, such as the Clouded Sulfur and the European Cabbage Butterfly, bask with their wings closed and their bodies aligned perpendicular to the sun.

Since basking butterflies are often more stationary than perching butterflies, they offer better opportunities for observation and photography. The Buckeye, for instance, spends a great deal of time basking in open, sandy areas, occasionally skipping from place to place.

Roosting

Butterflies need a place to roost for the night, and they often choose the underside of a leaf or a well-camouflaged portion of a bush. The best way to see where the butterflies are roosting is to wait until the very late afternoon and follow them to their roosting spot; this is a difficult, but not impossible, task. Butterflies also roost during cold, cloudy, or rainy weather. In general, they spend about 14 hours each day roosting, from late afternoon or sunset until midmorning the following day.

Strategies for Survival

Butterflies must defend themselves against a host of enemies and hazards, including birds, parasitic wasps, mantids, spiders, flies, inclement weather, and urban development. In their battle to survive, some butterflies have developed specific protective characteristics. For example, Buckeyes have evolved eyelike spots on the tips of their wings, which divert the

Top: Butterflies roost during cold and cloudy periods as well as during the night. Shown here is a roosting group of Orange-bordered Blues. Center: A Buckeye's eyespots lure predators, especially birds, away from the butterfly's vital parts. Bottom: The "tails" of swallowtails encourage birds to bite off this more accessible portion of the butterfly's wings, thereby saving crucial body parts from harm. Shown here is a Western Tiger Swallowtail on lilac.

attention of birds and thereby protect the butterfly's vital parts from being eaten. The "tails" of swallowtails perform a similar function in that they trick birds into biting off this more accessible portion of the butterfly's body, thus saving its vital parts from damage. From time to time, you may see a swallowtail missing a portion of its tail or perhaps a Buckeye with a missing wing tip.

Other butterflies use camouflage to blend into their background. The underwings of many anglewing species blend almost perfectly with the tree bark on which they perch, and the wings have uneven edges suggesting the border of a dead leaf.

Top: Some butterflies, such as this male Zephyr Anglewing, use camouflage as a means of protection from potential predators. Center: The Pipe Vine Swallowtail, a species distasteful to birds and other predators, is mimicked by the Spicebush Swallowtail (bottom), the female Tiger Swallowtail, the female Black Swallowtail, and other species.

Still other butterflies mimic the appearance of species that are distasteful to predators. The Viceroy mimics the orange and black Monarch; and some swallowtails, such as the Tiger, Spicebush, and Black swallowtails, mimic the coloring of the Pipe Vine Swallowtail. The very similar appearances of these butterflies can make accurate identification of these butterflies difficult.

Hibernation and Migration

Some butterflies, such as the Mourning Cloak and the anglewings, spend the winter as adults hibernating in the crevices of tree trunks and walls. These butterflies emerge from the pupa in early summer or early fall, and after flying around until late fall, they seek a sheltered spot, such as a hollow tree or a vacant shed, in which to pass the colder months of the year in relative safety. If you have such species in your garden, you may see one of them flying out on a warm winter day in search of food.

The Monarch is the only truly migratory butterfly. It escapes life-threatening cold weather by traveling as many as two thousand miles from its summer range throughout North America to overwintering sites in central Mexico and on the California coast. Monarchs from the East and Midwest travel to a small region of fir forests in central Mexico for the winter; Monarchs in the far West travel to pine and eucalyptus groves along the coast of California to escape the cold temperatures of the north that would kill them.

Perhaps the most amazing aspect of the Monarchs' migration is that they have never been to the areas to which they migrate. Monarchs that travel south in the fall have only just emerged from their pupae. Likewise, the Monarchs that migrate to the northern areas in the spring are perhaps the second or third generation after those that last overwintered in the south, mated in the spring, and then perished shortly thereafter along their journey northward. It is a mystery how these butterflies know where to go.

Some butterflies engage in one-way emigrations, taking advantage of the summer heat to expand their range northward. Notable among these species are the Cloudless Sulfur, Sleepy Orange, Variegated Fritillary, Gulf Fritillary, and Buckeye. Cold northern winters later kill these colonists.

Depending on the region in which you live and the habits of the various butterflies that reside in or pass through your area, you may see certain species on the wing at various times during much of the year. The complexity and variety of butterfly behavior is part of the fun of having a butterfly garden.

Monarchs migrate hundreds of miles each year to central Mexico, where they pass the winter clinging to tree branches in clusters of a million or more.

DESIGNING A BUTTERFLY GARDEN

A successful butterfly garden is one that contains all the components that butterflies need for food, shelter, and breeding, while providing the beauty of design and planting that appeal to the gardener. Butterflies need sunlight to keep their bodies working effectively; a food source and water to give them energy and nutrients for their activities; and hospitable surroundings that offer cover from the elements, a place to spend the night, and, in general, approximate the environment of their natural world. The environment must be stable and predictable, so that the needs of butterflies are met consistently over time. Balancing these components is part of the challenge and the art of butterfly gardening.

NECTAR FLOWERS

The successful butterfly garden offers both nectar flowers and roosting places. Here a Giant Swallowtail takes nectar from a bougainvillea.

Flower nectar is a primary food source for most butterflies. Butterflies take nectar from a wide variety of annuals, perennials, shrubs, trees, vines, and herbs. Fortunately, the flowers that butterflies favor for food are often the same ones that gardeners choose for their beauty or fragrance.

Nectar flowers can easily be incorporated into the garden in an aesthetically pleasing manner that satisfies both the butterfly's need for nectar and the gardener's desire for attractive flowers. A large patch of purple coneflower (*Echinacea*) for summer color; a border of red, white, or blue phlox (*Phlox*); or a trellis covered with the violet-blue blossoms of a wisteria (*Wisteria*) vine—there are so many nectar flowers that provide food for the butterflies and suit a wide range of garden designs.

In general, the more of a given nectar flower that is in bloom, the more likely butterflies will be to select it for its nectar. To make the most of the butterfly-attracting capabilities of nectar flowers it's best to plant them in patches rather than as isolated plants. Massed nectar flowers provide a large area of color or a strong scent that will attract the butterflies. Also, the larger the number of nectar-brimming blossoms, the longer the butterflies will stay in your garden.

Flower Shapes

Nectar flowers exist in many forms and shapes, some uniquely suited to the feeding needs of the butterfly. Composites have a wide platform

Butterfly Garden—Plan View

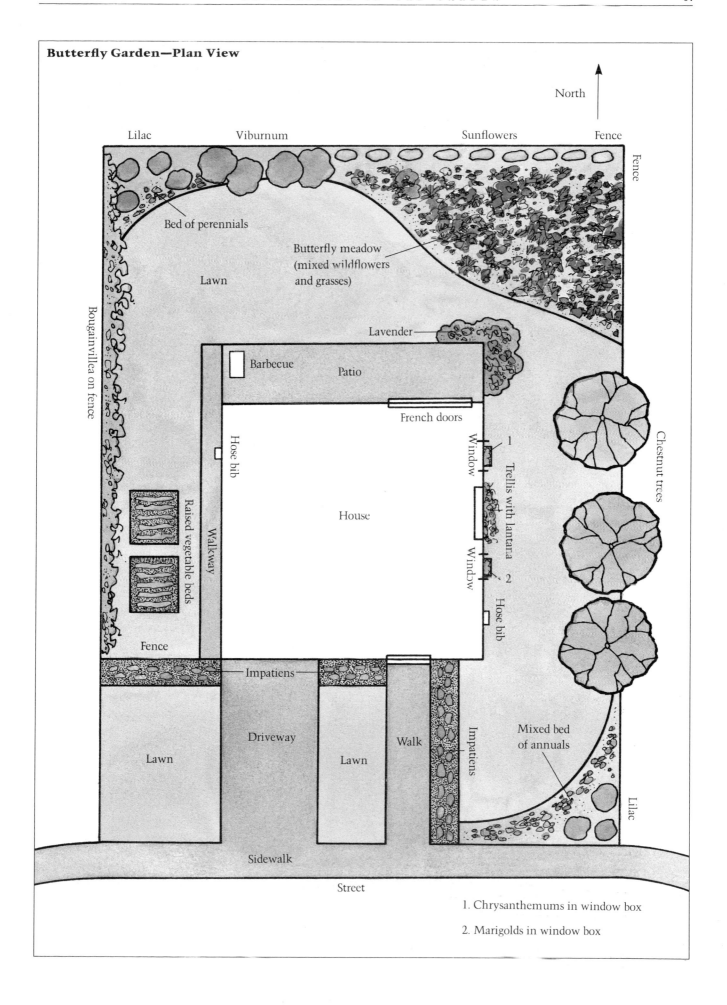

North

Lilac

Viburnum

Sunflowers

Fence

Fence

Bed of perennials

Butterfly meadow
(mixed wildflowers
and grasses)

Lawn

Bougainvillea on fence

Lavender

Barbecue

Patio

French doors

Window

1

Trellis with lantara

Hose bib

House

Window

2

Hose bib

Raised vegetable beds

Walkway

Chestnut trees

Fence

Impatiens

Impatiens

Mixed bed
of annuals

Lawn

Driveway

Lawn

Walk

Lilac

Sidewalk

Street

1. Chrysanthemums in window box

2. Marigolds in window box

Zinnias, composed of many small blossoms, are an example of the composite flower type, a type that is popular with butterflies.

Right: Plants with closely packed clusters of flowers—such as this lantana—are another favorite nectar source for butterflies. Bottom: Honeysuckle vines, with their many individual nectar-providing blossoms, are an important food source for butterflies.

on which butterflies perch while they take nectar from the many individual small flowers. Composites include daisies (*Bellis*), marigolds (*Tagetes*), and shepherd's-needle (*Bidens pilosa*). Other nectar flowers, butterfly bush (*Buddleia davidii*) for example, are composed of closely packed clusters of flowers arranged in spikes or, like the butterfly weed (*Asclepias tuberosa*), in broad umbels (an umbrellalike flower cluster in which all the flower stalks emerge from one central point). Some, such as honeysuckle (*Lonicera*), are borne on vines, and spread evenly across the surface of the plant. Still others, such as daylilies (*Hemerocallis*), are large single flowers to which butterflies cling while they feed.

Flower Plantings

The many nectar flower shapes and colors provide a variety of choices for creative butterfly garden designs: a long, wide patch of gloriosa daisies (*Rudbeckia hirta*) along a pathway; an open area in a corner with a tall butterfly bush

A Natural Garden

A natural setting for butterflies is both attractive and essential to their well-being. Although your plants may suffer some damage by hungry larvae, pesticides and herbicides should not be used in a butterfly garden. Chemicals will kill off adult butterflies that have found their way into the garden as well as eggs and larvae that are developing into adults.

Pesticides and herbicides are also toxic to beneficial insects that control pests—and butterflies—naturally. There are a sufficient number of these natural predators to maintain a good balance without using chemical measures. Natural predators such as spiders and birds will usually keep the larva population in check. Many butterfly larvae and pupae will also fall prey to parasitic flies and wasps that lay their eggs in them; the emerging fly and wasp larvae destroy the butterfly larvae and pupae by eating them from within. If you are concerned about larvae on edible crops, you can perhaps simply pick them off your vegetables and place them on other acceptable host plants in the neighborhood. Despite all these natural dangers, enough butterflies should survive to adulthood to amply supply your garden, provided you do not use chemical controls.

(*Buddleia davidii*), its purple or white spikes attracting butterflies from all sides; or a low border of purple ageratum (*Ageratum houstonianum*) and white sweet alyssum (*Lobularia maritima*) that draw the eye toward pink spikes of astilbe (*Astilbe*) behind them. The broad, orange flower heads of butterfly weed (*Asclepias tuberosa*) create a soft, almost delicate look to the garden, especially when planted in large patches. Daylilies (*Hemerocallis*) spread in various places around the garden provide an effective accent of shape and color that complements other flowers.

Lay out a row of lavender bushes (*Lavandula*) or a bed of many-colored impatiens (*Impatiens*) flowers. A row of tall yellow or gold sunflowers (*Helianthus*) will vary the vertical plane of the garden while also providing butterflies a good nectar target within their flight path. Some butterfly species, such as the Tiger Swallowtail and Spring Azure, visit tall flowers; other species, such as the Little Sulfur and the Least Skipper, stay close to the ground in their search for nectar. Planning your butterfly garden around the feeding habits of your favorite butterflies will one day provide the pleasure of seeing one coming into the garden to take nectar from a flower that you planted for it.

Top: A varied and colorful bed of sweet-william, black-eyed-susan, dahlia, and other nectar flowers provides butterflies with food, shelter, and a place to bask in the sun.
Bottom left: The large, single flower of the daylily is another nectar source preferred by butterflies.
Bottom right: Color, massed plantings, and sheltering shrubs are important aspects of butterfly-garden design. This garden contains purple coneflower and butterfly weed, as well as beebalm, a hummingbird flower.

Top: Glossy abelia, daylilies, and sweet alyssum offer a protected spot and nectar flowers for butterflies, and create an attractive lawn border.
Bottom: A group of flowers rather than a single stem provides butterflies with a greater and more efficient concentration of nectar. Here, an American Painted Lady takes nectar from a zinnia.

For butterfly gardeners who enjoy daisylike flowers, planting an entire front- or backyard bank of yellow-and-black gloriosa daisies (*Rudbeckia hirta*), purple coneflowers (*Echinacea purpurea*), yellow-and-red gaillardia (*Gaillardia*), and perhaps pink or white chrysanthemums (*Chrysanthemum*) will provide a wide expanse of color to attract the butterflies. It will also provide a spectacular floral display for your own enjoyment.

Flowers for Shelter

Because butterflies thrive better in a sheltered garden than in one exposed to wind, plant tall shrubs, vines, or trees around the perimeter of the garden to provide a windbreak. If possible, select plants that provide nectar as well as shelter for the butterflies.

Pink or white viburnum (*Viburnum*) bushes are an excellent choice for lining the perimeter of a butterfly garden. A wall or trellis covered with yellow or white honeysuckle (*Lonicera*) or purple wisteria (*Wisteria*) will work as well. Plant cherry, chestnut, pear, or plum trees on the boundaries too. All of these plants will serve as windbreaks while also providing nectar.

Flower Fragrances

Lantana (*Lantana*), butterfly bush (*Buddleia davidii*), honeysuckle (*Lonicera*), sweet alyssum (*Lobularia maritima*), pink (*Dianthus*), and wallflower (*Cheiranthus cheiri*) all have strong, sweet fragrances that attract and appeal to both butterflies and people. Butterflies are often much more attracted to sweetly scented flowers than they are to other flowers in the garden. For example, butterfly bush, with its strong scent, is often covered with butterflies taking nectar from its fragrant blossoms. Other nectar flowers that exude a strong scent that attracts butterflies even from a distance include lilac (*Syringa*), lavender (*Lavandula*), heliotrope (*Heliotropium arborescens)*, and mockorange (*Philadelphus*).

Flower Seasons

Another factor to consider in planning a butterfly garden is the timing and length of each plant's flowering season. Because butterflies require nectar during the entire season they are present in the garden, choose a selection of plants that blossom at different times to provide a continuous supply of nectar. In this way, you will keep the butterflies well fed and ensure they remain longer in your garden. In the cold areas of the country, where butterflies are not on the wing during the winter months, you will need a number of nectar flowers in bloom from spring to fall. In warm winter areas, where many butterflies are on the wing throughout the year, provide blooming flowers during the winter as well.

Left: Lantana provides nectar for butterflies and also brings an appealing fragrance and color to the garden.
Right: Provide nectar flowers as much as possible throughout the year. Lilacs are attractive early bloomers with fragrant nectar flowers.

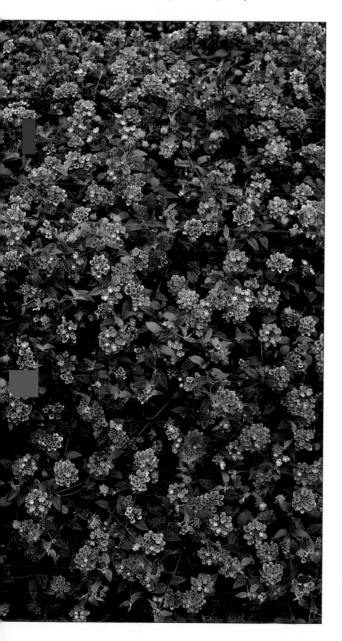

Impatiens are an important nectar source; they bloom all summer.

Goldenrod is a late-blooming butterfly nectar source.

In the cold winter regions of the country, early-spring bloomers like rockcress (*Arabis*) and lilac (*Syringa*) will attract butterflies such as the Spring Azure. Follow these plants with summer bloomers—cornflower (*Centaurea cyanus*) and impatiens (*Impatiens*)—and follow these in turn with late bloomers, such as butterfly bush (*Buddleia davidii*) and goldenrod (*Solidago*). In the warm winter areas of the country, long-blooming flowers like lantana (*Lantana*) and bougainvillea (*Bougainvillea*) will provide nectar throughout the year.

Annuals, such as ageratum (*Ageratum*), cosmos (*Cosmos*), and marigold (*Tagetes*), often have a long blooming season. Annuals also allow you to change the look of the flower beds from season to season and are ideal for flowerpots and hanging baskets.

Perennials, such as aster (*Aster*), goldenrod (*Solidago*), and primrose (*Primula*), offer the convenience of being around year after year. Biennials, such as echium (*Echium*) and wallflower (*Cheiranthus cheiri*), will survive for several blooming seasons.

SHELTER

Butterflies require shelter from the wind, rain, and other elements, as well as a place to roost at night. Providing shelter for butterflies will go a long way toward keeping them in the garden. Shrub foliage is not only useful as a windbreak, it also offers butterflies a protected spot to roost for the night. Exposed bare branches are a perfect place from which to foray out on courtship flights.

Some butterflies will also perch and roost in overgrown areas and patches of tall grass. In one area of the garden let the grass grow tall and the flowers grow naturally without trimming. An overgrown area will resemble the butterfly's natural habitat and provide more protection from the elements than a single flower border next to a lawn.

Butterfly Log Pile

Another way to provide a place for butterflies to perch, roost, or even hibernate is to build an open structure of logs. Place the logs crosswise—log cabin style—to create as many open spaces within the pile as possible. The log pile should be about 3 to 5 feet high, and the logs about 3 to 6 feet long, depending on the space you have available. Cover the top of the log pile to protect the butterflies from rain. By using thin logs, you can create more layers, and therefore more cavities for the butterflies.

Place the log pile in the shade (preferable for hibernating butterflies so that they do not get too hot and possibly perish), and plant nectar flowers and host plants nearby to attract the butterflies. Also, since the larvae of some species, such as the Tiger Swallowtail, leave their host plant to pass through the pupal stage, a log pile built near host plants will sometimes attract larvae away from the host plants when they are ready to pupate.

A log pile provides a comfortable sanctuary for butterfly roosting and hibernation.

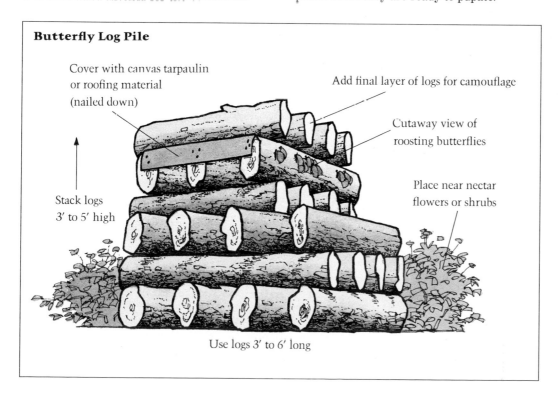

Butterfly Log Pile

Cover with canvas tarpaulin or roofing material (nailed down)

Add final layer of logs for camouflage

Cutaway view of roosting butterflies

Stack logs 3' to 5' high

Place near nectar flowers or shrubs

Use logs 3' to 6' long

Butterfly hibernation houses can be built or purchased commercially. The openings are just large enough for a butterfly to pass through but small enough to keep predators out.

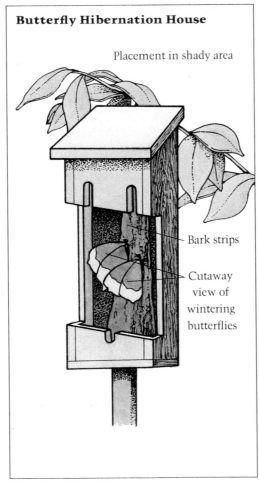

Butterfly Hibernation House

Placement in shady area

Bark strips

Cutaway view of wintering butterflies

Butterfly Hibernation House

Some hibernating butterflies are present during the winter in all parts of North America: the Mourning Cloak hibernates in many regions, the Question Mark and Comma in the East, and the Satyr Anglewing in the West. These overwintering species need a suitable spot for hibernating, which you can easily provide. To build a butterfly hibernation house, start with a rectangular wooden box with narrow vertical holes cut into it for the butterflies to enter and leave. Place long strips of bark inside the box to give the butterflies something to cling to. Coffee cans also make good hibernation houses; place them strategically in shrubs or trees and line them with tree bark or something that the butterflies can cling to. Always place a hibernation house in a shady area of the garden, so that the butterflies won't become overheated inside.

SUNSHINE

Warm sunshine is an essential ingredient of any butterfly garden; without it, the butterflies cannot fly and forage for nectar. Ideally, a butterfly garden should have a southern exposure so that it receives the maximum sunlight throughout the day. Provide ample open space in the garden, preferably in the center, so that the butterflies have adequate room to fly about and catch the rays of the sun. In large gardens, approximate the natural appearance of a forest glade or mountain meadow by leaving an open, sunny area among the shrubbery and trees.

Nectar flowers need to be in areas of near-continuous sun. Butterflies are more likely to fly to flowers placed in the sun than to those placed in the shade. Most nectar flowers thrive in full sun, so setting them out in the sunniest areas of the garden will be best for the butterflies and for the plants. In addition, females often lay their eggs on host plants that are placed in the sun.

MUD-PUDDLING

Swallowtails, sulfurs, blues, skippers, and other butterflies obtain moisture and essential nutrients and minerals from the moist areas around water. This practice is commonly known as mud-puddling. Streams and ponds, either natural or artificial, are distinct assets to a butterfly garden, since they are both attractive and practical. Start a mud-puddle club of Tiger

Include open, sunny areas in the garden so that butterflies can fly freely. Butterflies require air temperatures of at least 60° F for flight.

Left: Some butterflies, such as these Tiger and Palamedes swallowtails, gather in mud-puddle clubs to obtain moisture from damp ground.
Right: Butterflies raise their body temperature by basking either with their wings spread (like this Painted Lady) or with their wings closed and one side perpendicular to the sun.

Swallowtails or Clouded Sulfurs by allowing a damp area or shallow puddle to form in the garden. Add salt to the water from time to time to provide mud-puddling butterflies with the sodium they need.

Mud-puddle clubs are usually composed of young patrolling males out searching for a receptive mate. You can expect to see such mud-puddling butterflies as the European Cabbage Butterfly, Spicebush Swallowtail, and Orange Sulfur just after the emergence of each new generation during the year.

Mud-puddling usually occurs during the warmest hours of the day, generally between 10 a.m. and 2 p.m. The butterflies, rather than landing directly on the puddle, will gather on the moist dirt or sand on the side of the puddle to obtain moisture without putting themselves in any danger.

BASKING

Consider including a flat, rocky area in your garden, where butterflies can bask in the sun while absorbing the warmth of the rocks. A south-facing gradual slope is ideal for a basking spot. Imbed several flat rocks in the soil and watch for butterflies as they come to bask.

With the rocks in place, you are only one step away from a butterfly rock garden—plant ground cover nectar flowers, such as sweet alyssum (*Lobularia maritima*) or rockcress (*Arabis*), among the rocks and low-growing host plants such as nasturtium (*Tropaeolum*) and clover (*Trifolium*), for the larvae.

Butterflies will also use brick or cement patios, wooden decks, or even gravel or dirt paths for basking. Place nectar flowers such as impatiens (*Impatiens*) and phlox (*Phlox*) in pots near these areas and potted host plants, too.

Successful butterfly gardening can be done on a small scale. This patio container has an array of butterfly flowers—petunias, lobelia, sweet alyssum—in addition to sage, a favorite of hummingbirds.

CONTAINER PLANTS

Potted butterfly flowers bring a great deal of versatility to butterfly gardening. You can move them around on the patio, bring potted cold-sensitive plants inside for the winter, or set up a butterfly container garden in a small urban space.

Consider using impatiens (*Impatiens*) in hanging baskets on the end of a trellis, or phlox (*Phlox*) either in large pots in the sitting area of a gazebo or in hanging baskets on the outside of the structure. Other nectar flowers that lend themselves well to container gardening include ageratum (*Ageratum*), cosmos (*Cosmos*), daylily (*Hemerocallis*), primrose (*Primula*), and even shrubs such as butterfly bush

(*Buddleia davidii*), lilac (*Syringa*), and viburnum (*Viburnum*). A group of container plants massed in one area of your garden is more likely to attract and keep the butterflies than scattered, individual containers. Like their garden counterparts, container plants need to be in the sun so that butterflies will be more likely to fly to them.

If there's an opportunity to place potted plants quite near a picture window, you will be able to identify visiting butterflies and observe their behavior and activity up close. Alternatively, planting small nectar flowers, such as ageratum (*Ageratum*) and impatiens (*Impatiens*), in a window box may entice butterflies to within inches of the window.

A BUTTERFLY MEADOW

Butterflies are attracted to open areas of grass and wildflowers that resemble their natural habitats. A butterfly meadow can be both a simple means of attracting butterflies and an aesthetically pleasing addition to the garden.

Let a part of your yard grow wild, preferably with grasses and wildflowers that are native to the area. Some wildflower favorites that will serve as excellent nectar flowers throughout North America are thistle (*Cirsium*), dandelion (*Taraxacum*), knapweed (*Centaurea*), fleabane (*Erigeron*), and clover (*Trifolium*). Eastern butterfly gardeners can add joe-pye-weed (*Eupatorium*) or ironweed (*Vernonia*); butterfly gardeners in the West might want to add centaury (*Centaurium*) or wild-lilac (*Ceanothus*). Wild varieties of goldenrod (*Solidago*), milkweed (*Asclepias*), phlox (*Phlox*), yarrow (*Achillea*), and sunflower (*Helianthus*) are also effective in a butterfly meadow.

By approximating the appearance of a butterfly's natural habitat, you have an excellent chance of attracting butterflies. Mix in host plants so that the females can lay their eggs in a natural setting alongside their favorite nectar flowers.

If your garden is adjacent to a natural area, you can enjoy the best of both worlds by extending your garden toward the natural area with native plantings and having cultivated flowers within the formal part of the garden. A small meadow area in a suburban or even an urban garden can bring a touch of the country and a contingent of butterflies to an otherwise cultivated yard. Even an apartment balcony can attract butterflies: Plant wildflowers in pots or in hanging baskets.

Butterfly meadows can be an attractive addition to a garden designed with butterflies in mind. Shown here is a prairie wildflower garden filled with butterfly weed, purple coneflower, and black-eyed-susan.

PROVIDING HOST PLANTS FOR LARVAE

Once you have attracted adult butterflies to your garden with the right conditions, encourage them to stay from generation to generation by providing the proper host plants. You can provide enough host plants for the butterfly larvae and still have plenty left for your own enjoyment. Place host plants in a wildflower meadow, next to a log pile that serves as a shelter or hibernation spot for butterflies, or in a special area of flower beds.

Quite a few butterflies are named for their favorite host plants, and these plants can be depended upon to attract their namesakes: Lure the Pipe Vine Swallowtail with pipe vine (*Aristolochia*), the Spicebush Swallowtail with spicebush (*Lindera benzoin*), the European Cabbage Butterfly with members of the cabbage family, the Orange Sulfur (or Alfalfa Sulfur) with alfalfa (*Medicago sativa*), and the Monarch (a member of the group of milkweed butterflies) with milkweed (*Asclepias*).

Various carrot family members, such as Queen-Anne's-lace (*Daucus carota*) and parsley (*Petroselinum crispum*) will attract the

Top: Some butterflies are named for their favorite host or nectar plants. The Monarch is one of the milkweed butterflies.
Bottom: Hibiscus is a favored host plant of the Gray Hairstreak.

Some butterflies obtain nutrients from food sources other than nectar flowers, as with this Red Admiral feeding on an apple.

Black Swallowtail; in the West the Anise Swallowtail will flit into your yard for a generous planting of fennel (*Foeniculum vulgare*). The Gray Hairstreak uses many different types of host plants, such as clover (*Trifolium*), hibiscus (*Hibiscus*), and mallow (*Malva*). The Painted Lady also uses a wide variety of host plants, including thistle (*Cirsium*), common mallow (*Malva neglecta*), and hollyhock (*Alcea*). The Gulf Fritillary, however, chooses only various species of passion vine (*Passiflora*), and the Great Spangled Fritillary limits its larval feeding to various types of violets (*Viola*).

In general, the host plants that you provide for your favorite butterflies will attract only those specific butterflies. And, in most cases, the larvae will leave other garden plants untouched.

Protecting Host Plants

To protect certain host plant vegetables and herbs, such as cabbage, parsley, dill, and alfalfa, from being eaten by the larvae of butterflies, put netting over one area of the crop and leave another area exposed for the butterflies to use. The netting will prevent the females from laying their eggs on the particular host plants that you want to protect.

Integrating Host Plants

Host plants need never be simply plants for butterfly larvae. Host-plant vines, such as passion vine (*Passiflora*) and pipe vine (*Aristolochia*), make excellent wall, fence, and trellis coverings; host trees, such as cherry or ash (favorites of the Tiger Swallowtail), planted in rows can serve as an effective windbreak and shelter area.

Pearly everlasting (*Anaphalis margaritacea*) and fennel (*Foeniculum vulgare*) will add a light touch of greenery and white and yellow clusters of flowers, respectively, to your garden; and thistle (*Cirsium*) and milkweed (*Asclepias*) yield very popular nectar flowers as well as attract female Painted Ladies and Monarchs, respectively, to lay their eggs.

PROVIDING OTHER FOOD SOURCES

Instead of flower nectar, some butterflies—the Mourning Cloak, Red Admiral, and Viceroy among them—feed primarily on rotting fruit,

Butterfly feeders may be made out of materials at hand. Here, plastic kitchen scouring pads provide a place for a Giant Swallowtail to perch while taking sugar-water solution.

method is to place several plastic kitchen scouring pads (see photograph at left) in a dish to give the butterflies a place to perch while they drink. To stop harmful mold from forming, replace the sugar water and wash the dish thoroughly on a regular basis (once a week should be fine in moderate weather; twice a week in warm months).

Place the butterfly feeder near nectar flowers on a post 4 to 6 inches higher than the tallest flowers. The flowers will attract butterflies and the feeder will stand out, drawing the butterflies to the alternative food source. Use butterfly feeders during late fall to early spring, when nectar flowers are least abundant. Feeders are especially handy for hibernating butterflies when they emerge in search of food on warm, sunny winter days.

To protect butterfly feeders from ants, bees, wasps, and other insects that will compete with butterflies for the food, place sticky tape on the post below the feeder. Another alternative is to place petroleum jelly or salad or mineral oil on or around the feeder to prevent unwanted insects from getting a foothold.

Butterfly Tables

Equally attractive to butterflies are butterfly tables stocked with dishes of sugar water and rotting fruit. Once butterflies pick up the odor of the fruit, they will find the table and remain to eat. Place the table about 4 or 5 feet off the ground to make it available to butterflies and less accessible to ants and other insects. As with butterfly feeders, use various sticky and slippery substances to help prevent ants, bees, and wasps from taking the food.

ENJOYING THE BUTTERFLY GARDEN

Butterfly gardening can involve much more than just watching the butterflies that find their way into your garden—it can provide a way to interact more closely with nature as it unfolds in front of you. In addition to the hours of enjoyment observing the variety of butterflies in the garden, you may want to expand your activities in a number of areas.

Keeping a Journal

Keep a journal of butterfly activities on a daily or a seasonal basis. The information you record about butterfly behavior and preferences will

tree sap, and even dung and carrion, gaining moisture and nutrients from all these substances. Many of these butterflies (including anglewings, satyrs, and wood nymphs) live in forest environments, where there are relatively few flowers that provide nectar. Over the course of their evolution, these butterfly groups have adapted to making use of alternative sources of nourishment.

For these butterflies, set out a plate of rotting bananas, plums, pears, or other fruit to which you have added stale beer, sugar or molasses, and yeast. Allow the mixture to ferment. The mixture gives off a strong odor that will attract butterflies. You can even "paint" it on the trunks of trees to simulate tree sap.

Butterfly Feeders

A popular alternative food source for butterflies is homemade feeders filled with a solution of sugar water. Mix 4 parts water with 1 part white granulated sugar, boil the solution for several minutes until the sugar is dissolved, and let the solution cool. Store extra solution in the refrigerator—it will keep for up to a week.

Make the butterfly feeder by filling a dish or other flat container with an absorbent material such as tissue paper and saturating the material with the sugar solution. Another

help you to learn how to enhance the garden and increase your success at attracting and keeping butterflies. A journal might also lead to some interesting discoveries—perhaps a new choice of host plant for a particular butterfly or a new type of hibernation spot.

Try your hand at butterfly photography or drawing. There is perhaps nothing quite as rewarding in butterfly gardening as capturing on film one of your favorite butterflies at one of its favorite flowers.

Raising Butterflies

A popular butterfly gardening activity is rearing butterflies from the egg to the adult stage, and then letting them go. Butterfly raising is often done indoors. Place small branches or stems of the butterfly's host plant, with eggs attached, in a jar of water, and place the jar in a small box. The water contained in the jar will nourish the plant while the eggs hatch, and retain the greenery for the emerging larvae to eat. Make sure that the section of plant where the eggs are attached is above the jar's mouth. Next, cover the open box with a closely meshed net. Keep the top of the jar closed off so that the larvae won't crawl or fall into it. Place a stick upright in the box to provide the pupae something to hold onto. A cage is as effective as

a box, but be sure that the weave of the cage is fine enough that even the smallest larvae can't escape. Larvae raised in this way will eventually become pupae and hatch into adults. Rearing butterflies can be a very enjoyable and educational activity, allowing you to get close-up observations of butterflies in all stages of their life cycle.

Joining Up

Your interest in butterfly gardening might quickly develop into an interest in the butterflies themselves or the flowers that sustain them in the wild. If it does, join an entomological organization, such as the Lepidopterists' Society; a butterfly conservation group, such as the Xerces Society; or a wildflower conservation organization, such as the National Wildflower Research Center (see page 107). By becoming involved in the activities of organizations such as these, you may foster new realms of scientific discovery, help to preserve precious habitat, or contribute to the fund of knowledge on our most endangered wildflowers.

If you have no time to pursue these activities and all you do is observe butterflies taking nectar from their favorite flowers, the effort involved in starting your butterfly garden will still have been well worthwhile.

Butterflies can be raised in a variety of conditions—from this large butterfly house to glass jars in the home.

Achillea 'Moonshine' (yarrow)

Asclepias tuberosa (butterfly weed)

Aster × frikartii (aster)

BUTTERFLY PLANTS

Botanical and Common Names	Type And Size	Blooming Season	Flower Color(s)	Soil	Light	USDA Zone Adaptation
Achillea species Yarrow	Perennials	Spring–fall	Yellow, white, red	Well drained	Full sun	All
Ageratum houstonianum Ageratum, flossflower	Annual	Spring–fall	Blue, white, pink	Fertile, moist	Full sun	All
Arabis species Rockcress	Perennials	Spring	White, pink, purple	Sandy	Full sun	All
Asclepias tuberosa Butterfly weed, milkweed	Perennial	Summer	Orange	Well drained	Full sun	3–10
Aster species Aster	Perennials	Summer–fall	Blue, purple, red, pink, white	Moist	Full sun	4–10
Astilbe species Astilbe, false-spiraea, meadowsweet	Perennials	Summer	Red, white, pink	Rich, moist	Partial shade	4–10
Bougainvillea species Bougainvillea	Evergreen vines	Almost year around	Various	Any	Full sun	9, 10
Buddleia davidii Common butterfly bush, summer-lilac	Deciduous or semievergreen shrub to 10′	Late summer–early fall	Lavender, blue, white	Alkaline	Full sun	5–9
Centaurea cyanus Cornflower, bachelor's-button	Annual	Summer	Blue, purple, pink, white, red	Moist	Full sun	All
Cheiranthus cheiri Wallflower	Biennial, perennial	Spring–summer	Yellow, orange, red, purple	Moist	Full sun	8–10

Centaurea cyanus 'Bluc Boy' (cornflower)

Dahlia 'Cup o' Tea' (dahlia)

Chrysanthemum × *superbum* (Shasta daisy)

BUTTERFLY PLANTS

Botanical and Common Names	Type And Size	Blooming Season	Flower Color(s)	Soil	Light	USDA Zone Adaptation
Chrysanthemum species Chrysanthemum	Annuals, perennials	Summer–fall	Various	Well drained	Full sun	All
Coreopsis species Coreopsis	Annuals, perennials	Spring–fall	Yellow, orange, red, purple, pink, bicolors	Well drained	Full sun	All
Cosmos species Cosmos	Annuals	Summer–fall	White, pink, purple, red, yellow, lavender	Well drained	Full sun	All
Dahlia species Dahlia	Perennials	Summer–fall	Various	Well drained	Full sun	All
Dianthus species Pink	Annuals, biennials, perennials	Spring–fall	Various	Well drained	Full sun	All
Echinacea purpurea Purple coneflower	Perennial	Summer	Purple	Well drained	Full sun	3–10
Echinops exaltatus Globethistle	Perennial	Summer–fall	Blue	Well drained	Full sun	3–10
Echium species Echium	Biennials, perennials	Spring	Blue, white, pink, red, purple	Well drained	Full sun	8–10
Gaillardia species Gaillardia	Annuals, perennials	Spring–fall	Red, orange, yellow	Well drained	Full sun	All
Helianthus species Sunflower	Annuals, perennials	Summer–fall	Yellow, orange	Well drained	Full sun	All
Hemerocallis species Daylily	Perennials	Spring–fall	Various	Most	Full sun	3–10

Dianthus barbatus (sweet-william)

Gaillardia pulchella (gaillardia)

BUTTERFLY PLANTS

Botanical and Common Names	Type And Size	Blooming Season	Flower Color(s)	Soil	Light	USDA Zone Adaptation
Iberis species Candytuft	Annuals, perennials	Spring–summer	White, purple, pink, red	Moist	Full sun	All
Impatiens species Impatiens, touch-me-not	Annuals, perennials	Summer	Various	Moist, acid	Full sun or partial shade	All
Lantana species Lantana	Evergreen shrubs to 6′	Year around	Red, orange, yellow, pink, purple, white	Most	Full sun	8–10
Lavandula species Lavender	Evergreen shrubs to 3′–4′	Year around	Lavender, purple	Well drained	Full sun	8–10
Lobelia species Lobelia	Annuals, perennials	Summer–fall	Blue, red, purple, white	Rich, moist	Full sun or partial shade	All
Lobularia maritima Sweet alyssum	Annual	Year around (spring–fall in colder climates)	White, pink, purple	Well drained	Full sun	All
Lonicera species Honeysuckle	Evergreen or semievergreen vines	Spring–fall	Yellow, red, white, pink, purple	Well drained, loamy	Full sun or partial shade	3–9
Petunia × *hybrida* Petunia	Perennial often used as an annual	Spring–summer	Various	Well drained, light	Full sun	All
Phlox species Phlox	Annuals, perennials	Spring–summer	Various	Moist	Full sun	All
Primula species Primrose	Perennials	Spring–summer	Various	Moist	Partial shade	5–10
Rhododendron species Rhododendron, azalea	Evergreen or deciduous shrubs (sizes vary with variety)	Spring–summer	Various	Well drained	Full sun to partial shade	5–10

Tagetes 'Lemon Gem' (marigold)

Rudbeckia hirta (black-eyed-susan, gloriosa daisy)

Viburnum plicatum (Japanese snowball viburnum)

BUTTERFLY PLANTS

Botanical and Common Names	Type And Size	Blooming Season	Flower Color(s)	Soil	Light	USDA Zone Adaptation
Rudbeckia hirta Black-eyed-susan, gloriosa daisy	Biennial, perennial	Summer–fall	Yellow, orange, red	Most	Full sun	All
Scabiosa species Pincushion-flower, scabious	Annuals, perennials	Summer–fall	Purple, pink, white, red, blue	Well drained	Full sun	All
Sedum spectabile Showy stonecrop	Perennial	Summer–fall	Pink, red	Well drained	Full sun	3–10
Solidago species Goldenrod	Perennials	Summer–fall	Yellow	Average	Full sun	3–10
Syringa species Lilac	Deciduous shrubs or small trees to 8′–12′ (depending on variety)	Spring	Purple, white, lavender, pink	Well drained	Full sun	3–7
Tagetes species Marigold	Annuals	Summer–fall	Yellow, orange, red	Moist	Full sun	All
Verbena species Verbena	Annuals, perennials	Spring–fall	White, pink, purple, red, blue, yellow	Well drained	Full sun	All
Viburnum species Viburnum	Deciduous or evergreen shrubs or small trees (sizes vary with variety)	Year around	White, pink	Moist	Sun or shade	3–10
Wisteria species Wisteria	Deciduous vines	Spring	Purple, blue, white, pink	Well drained	Full sun	5–10
Zinnia species Zinnia	Annuals	Summer–fall	Various	Well drained	Full sun	All

Gallery of Hummingbirds and Butterflies

The galleries in this chapter describe and feature photographs of the most commonly found hummingbirds and butterflies. They will help you to identify and understand a wide range of species and to provide for their needs.

The descriptions that follow discuss the eight most common hummingbird species that range well northward into the United States and Canada and two others—the Blue-throated and Magnificent hummingbirds—that breed in mountainous areas just across the border between the United States and Mexico. Not included here are the Broad-billed, White-eared, Berylline, Buff-bellied, Violet-crowned, and Lucifer hummingbirds. Although these six are of special interest, they nevertheless have limited ranges and, for the most part, are difficult to find.

The 10 species included in this gallery, like all hummingbirds, are members of the same family and, as such, are listed alphabetically (by common name). Each description mentions the key habits and characteristics of the hummingbird in question to help you identify it and provide the right conditions in your garden. Included is a description of the range in which the bird is found and a general description of its appearance and size (given in inches and referring to overall length). Following this are details of its habitat, nesting behaviors, and a list of its favorite nectar plants. All hummingbird descriptions are accompanied by a photograph and a map showing the areas in which each species is found. For more detailed information about each hummingbird's range, check a local field guide.

This garden includes butterfly plants (azalea) and hummingbird plants (flowering maple, camellia) and a hummingbird feeder. Impatiens appeal to both hummingbirds and butterflies.
Inset: Shown taking nectar from a fuchsia is a female Anna's Hummingbird.
Inset: A female American Painted Lady finds nourishment in a marigold.

Top: Red sage is favored by many hummingbirds, including the Blue-throated, the Allen's, and the Calliope. Bottom: It is not difficult to attract a variety of beautiful butterflies to the garden. Four species were sighted here when this photograph was taken.

A Guide to the Range Maps

For each hummingbird species featured in the gallery, the range maps that accompany each entry identify the breeding range, the winter range, and, for year-round residents, the permanent range. For each butterfly species, the maps show the permanent range where it is normally resident—in some form—the year around.

For the hummingbird range maps:

▪ breeding range

▪ winter range

▪ permanent range

For the butterfly range maps:

▪ permanent range

The butterfly gallery includes information about 26 of the most common nectar-feeding garden butterflies across the United States and Canada. The butterflies are grouped into families and listed taxonomically; that is, according to their natural relationships and evolutionary development. For alphabetical listings, refer to the index. In addition to information about each butterfly's range and background, flying season, favored host plants, and favorite nectar flowers, each entry describes the butterfly's habitats and distinguishing aspects of its behavior. The size measurements refer to the length of both forewings when spread (see illustration, page 59). As with the hummingbird gallery, each entry includes a range map. For more detailed information about each butterfly's range, check a local butterfly field guide.

The list of butterflies included here is a representative selection of butterflies with wide ranges and of various sizes, shapes, and colors. If you want to attract specific common local butterflies, consult the references listed in the back of this book (see page 107), related organizations, and local field guides.

To help you identify the butterflies, each entry features a photograph. Keep in mind, however, that male and female butterflies of the same species may vary in appearance, and sometimes individuals of the same sex and species will vary in appearance too—for example, albinism and other genetic differences, as well as seasonal and geographic variations affect the appearances of some species.

The more familiar you become with the physical traits, life cycle, habits, and favorite plants of the hummingbirds and butterflies in these galleries, the more successful you will be in attracting them to your garden.

Allen's Hummingbird (*Selasphorus sasin*)

Allen's Hummingbird

Selasphorus sasin

Range The Allen's Hummingbird is largely confined to coastal districts during the breeding season, nesting from the southwestern corner of Oregon to Ventura

County and the Channel Islands in southern California. A portion of the population departs for central Mexico during the summer and early fall migration period, but a slightly larger number are year-round residents of the Channel Islands and isolated spots in southern California. Small numbers winter in southeastern Arizona and along the Texas coast. The spring trek north from Mexico, which begins as early as January, is along the West Coast. The summer or early fall flight is by way of lower mountain slopes and foothills, where there are better opportunities for finding wildflowers.

Description The adult male has a green back and crown, an orange-red gorget, a white chest with cinnamon underparts, and a rufous (reddish) tail and rump. Except for the green back and crown, the male Allen's is identical to the male Rufous. The female Allen's has a green back and pale rufous sides. It so closely resembles the adult female Rufous, it is almost impossible to tell the two apart in the field. Size: 3⅓ inches.

Habitat Monterey pines, live oaks, redwoods, and eucalyptus trees are commonly chosen as nest sites in the moist coastal areas where the Allen's spends the breeding season. Normally nesting takes place away from human habitations, but there are records of nests on rafters, in vines on houses, and other similar sites. Once the nest is built, the Allen's freely enters yards and gardens.

Nesting The female occupies a separate territory from the male during the nesting season. She places her nest of fine rootlets, dry leaves, willow down, and hair at almost any height. The nest is held in place with spider webbing and camouflaged on the outside with lichens. The two white eggs, which may be laid as early as February, take 15 to 17 days to hatch. The young are in the nest for 22 to 25 days. Generally there will be one or two broods in a season. As part of his courtship behavior, a male Allen's performs aerial displays that typically consist of a pendulum arc complete with nosedives and tail and wing noises.

Favorite nectar plants The Allen's Hummingbird visits a wide variety of wildflowers and garden plants for nectar and insects. Among those commonly visited are California fuchsia (*Zauschneria californica*), cape-honeysuckle (*Tecomaria capensis*), century plant (*Agave americana*), American columbine (*Aquilegia canadensis*), Indian-paintbrush (*Castilleja coccinea*), madrone (*Arbutus menziesii*), monkeyflower (*Mimulus cardinalis*), scarlet sage (*Salvia splendens*), and tree tobacco (*Nicotiana glauca*).

Anna's Hummingbird

Calypte anna

Range Once restricted almost entirely to southern California, the slopes of the Sierra Nevada, and the San Francisco Bay Area, the Anna's, within the last 50 years, has been extending its range

southward, eastward, and northward. This increase in range has been triggered by suburban plantings, the spread of eucalyptus, and the presence of food at hummingbird feeders. The Anna's northward expansion has been particularly spectacular: The birds are breeding in coastal Oregon, Washington, and southwestern British Columbia, and sightings have occurred as far north as Alaska. Substantial numbers are now also breeding in Arizona. Each winter a few appear as far east as coastal Texas and Louisiana, suggesting that the Anna's is more of a migrator than had formerly been supposed.

Anna's Hummingbird (*Calypte anna*)

Black-chinned Hummingbird (*Archilochus alexandri*)

Nevertheless, a large proportion of the population remains in the breeding range throughout the year.

Description The male Anna's, with its distinctive iridescent rose gorget and crown, is unmistakable. When viewed from different angles, its brilliant coloring may appear violet, gold, or green. With the exception of the gorget and crown, the female Anna's is much like the male: bronzy green above and greenish white below. Size: 3½ to 4 inches.

Habitat During the breeding season, females nest in yards, chaparral thickets, wooded canyons, and low wooded slopes, often choosing groves of live oaks. Males tend to have separate territories in somewhat more open areas. The Anna's will often reside in well-planted yards the year around.

Nesting The earliest nester of any North American species, the Anna's may have eggs in the nest in December. Second and third nestings sometimes follow the first one. Nests are largely constructed of fine plant down and are securely held together with spider webbing. Feathers are

often used for lining the nest and lichens for camouflage on the outside. Nests are placed in a variety of locations, including outside lighting fixtures; the usual site is the upper side of a tree branch. The two pure white eggs take about 16 days to hatch. Young leave the nest in about three weeks.

As part of his courtship behavior and territorial defense, the male Anna's performs spectacular dive displays in which he rises to a height of as much as 120 feet and dives at a speed of up to 65 miles per hour. He also may perform a somewhat complex song, either from a perch or in flight.

Favorite nectar plants
Year-round blossoms are critical for this largely permanent resident. Favorites include coralbells (*Heuchera sanguinea*), eucalyptus (*Eucalyptus*), fuchsia (*Fuchsia*), flowering quince (*Chaenomeles*), fuchsia-flowered gooseberry (*Ribes speciosum*), lion's-tail (*Leonotis leonurus*), penstemon (*Penstemon*), pineapple sage (*Salvia elegans*), tree tobacco (*Nicotiana glauca*), and woolly bluecurls (*Trichostema lanatum*).

Black-chinned Hummingbird

Archilochus alexandri

Range This small hummingbird is often regarded as the western counterpart of its eastern relative, the Ruby-throated Hummingbird. The Black-chinned spends the warmer months in western

North America and winters in western Mexico. Its summer range extends from southern British Columbia and western Montana south through southern California, Arizona, New Mexico, and south-central Texas into northern Mexico. The species is largely absent west of the Cascades in Washington and Oregon and along the northern coastal region of California but is a common summer hummingbird in Arizona and also throughout much of the Southwest. In the fall the Black-chinned appears as far east as the northern Gulf Coast, and many remain there for the winter. Occasionally Black-chinneds are

seen in winter in southern California.

Description The female Black-chinned is iridescent green above and white below. The male has a solid black throat bordered by a narrow band of iridescent purple. A helpful clue in identifying the male Black-chinned is the distinctive whirring sound it makes with its wings when in flight. Size: 3⅛ to 3¾ inches.

Habitat The Black-chinned is found in both wild and semi-urban habitats. From hot, low-elevation cities it ranges upward to nearby mountain slopes.

Nesting Nesting sites are often in trees that line watercourses or dry creek beds. The nest is placed at a modest height in such trees as sycamore, cottonwood, oak, willow, or alder. Soft plant material like the yellowish down from the underside of sycamore leaves and the silky strands from milkweed seeds is commonly used in nest construction. The nest is held together and anchored with spider webbing. In urban habitats the Black-chinned makes use of ornamental trees and shrubs for nesting. It may also choose odd locations, such as a fold in

Blue-throated Hummingbird (*Lampornis clemenciae*)

a hanging coil of rope or the top of an outside lighting fixture, for a nesting site.

The two, sometimes three, eggs are incubated for around 16 days. Young stay in the nest about three weeks. Two or even three broods are reared during a nesting season, which normally lasts from April through August. (In contrast, most hummingbird species lay only two eggs and have one, sometimes two, broods.)

Favorite nectar plants The Black-chinned readily visits hummingbird feeders and the flowers of canna (*Canna*), century plant (*Agave americana*), chuparosa (*Justicia californica*), columbine (*Aquilegia*), garden balsam (*Impatiens balsamina*), paloverde (*Cercidium*), shrimpplant (*Justicia brandegeana*), tree tobacco (*Nicotiana glauca*), and yucca (*Yucca*).

Blue-throated Hummingbird

Lampornis clemenciae

Range This, the largest of North American hummingbirds, breeds in the mountains of southeastern Arizona, in southwestern New Mexico, and in the Chisos Mountains of western Texas. After the

breeding season, virtually the entire population returns to Mexico for the winter.

Description Their large, long wings and long, broad tails with conspicuous white tips at the outer feathers are helpful clues in identifying Blue-throated Hummingbirds of both sexes. Males are a dark metallic green on the upper parts. They have a blue gorget and a white stripe above and below the eye. Their underparts are gray. The female is similar to the male but lacks the blue gorget, and the facial stripes are less well defined. Size: 4½ to 5¼ inches.

Habitat Nesting territories are in wooded canyons and usually near streams. The female chooses a separate territory from the male, which stays at somewhat higher elevations, where wildflowers are more plentiful.

Nesting After the Blue-throated returns from Mexico in early spring, nesting gets under way. The nest is made in almost any place where overhead shelter is available. This includes under rock ledges, eaves, bridges, and water towers, beneath tree branches, and inside buildings. The nest, which is composed of plant fibers, cotton materials, mosses, and weed stems, is large for a North American hummingbird—up to 3 inches high and 2½ inches wide. It is held together with spider webbing.

The two eggs in a clutch hatch in 17 or 18 days. Young are in the nest from 24 to 29 days and on leaving resemble the adults. As many as three broods are reared during a nesting season, which lasts until August and sometimes as late as October.

Males defend their territory against intruders, especially other hummingbirds. During display flights, males fan their blackish tails, clearly showing the conspicuous white tips. They also deliver a squeaky song while perched.

Favorite nectar plants
Among the flowers most commonly visited are century plant (*Agave americana*), gilia (*Gilia*), lobelia (*Lobelia*), lupine (*Lupinus*), penstemon (*Penstemon*), scarlet sage (*Salvia splendens*), and tree tobacco (*Nicotiana glauca*).

Broad-tailed Hummingbird

Selasphorus platycercus

Range One of the most distinctive sounds in the Rockies in summer is the cricket trill that reverberates from the wings of the male Broad-tailed when it's in flight. The sound is heard throughout a wide

breeding range that extends from Idaho and western Wyoming southward through Nevada, Utah, western Colorado, eastern California, and through the mountains into Mexico.

When the Broad-tailed first begins arriving at its breeding range in April, it visits flowers at low elevations. But as flowers become abundant at higher

Broad-tailed Hummingbird (*Selasphorus platycercus*)

elevations, the Broad-tailed moves up into the mountains. Breeding has been recorded at up to 12,700 feet. After nesting, many Broad-tailed Hummingbirds make an altitudinal migration to above the timberline and begin working their way southward along mountaintops. Others fan out onto the Great Plains, some of them reaching the Texas and Louisiana coasts. Fall migration is completed by mid-October.

Description The tail of this species is broad and bronzy black. But more helpful identification clues are the wing buzz made by the male and his bright rose pink gorget. The male's green crown is also unique among North American hummingbirds. In both sexes the upper parts are a metallic green, merging into rich buff on the sides in the female and gray tinged with buff in the male. White is visible on the breast and underparts. Size: 4 to 4½ inches.

Habitat Rugged mountain terrain, with cliffs, canyons, and rushing streams, is the summer home of the Broad-tailed. Moving as it does from lower elevations to higher ones, the Broad-tailed has

adapted to whatever vegetational cover is present. This may be piñon pine and juniper at lower elevations, woodlands of pine and oak higher up, and aspen, Douglas fir, and ponderosa pine still higher. Nesting territories are near water and where wildflowers are abundant.

Nesting Except in the southernmost parts of its range, where nesting begins as early as late March, the normal nesting time is from late May until late July. The peak nesting period coincides with the blooming of favorite wildflowers. Nests are constructed of plant fibers, moss, shreds of bark, and down from the undersides of leaves.

It takes about 16 days for the two eggs to hatch. Young leave anywhere from 21 to 26 days after hatching. One or two broods are reared in a season.

For courtship and territorial defense, the male employs a variety of aerial displays: A courtship flight in which the male rises to a height of 20 to 40 feet and makes a U-shaped, shallow dive to intimidate a territorial rival. The male may also repeatedly circle his territory to protect it.

Favorite nectar plants
Among favored flowers are blue larkspur (*Delphinium scopulorum*), century plant (*Agave americana*), figwort (*Scrophularia*), gilia (*Gilia*), lousewort (*Pedicularis canadensis*), lupine (*Lupinus*), nasturtium (*Tropaeolum majus*), ocotillo (*Fouquieria splendens*), penstemon (*Penstemon*), and sage (*Salvia*).

Calliope Hummingbird

Stellula calliope

Range The Calliope is a bird of the mountainous regions of the West, breeding at elevations of up to 11,500 feet. Its breeding range extends from central British Columbia and southwestern Alberta, south

to western Colorado and Utah, and west to southern California and southern Nevada. Its winter range is in Mexico. The Calliope is less likely than

other western hummingbirds to stray to the East in the fall.

During spring migration, the Calliope times its flight northward with the blooming season of its favorite flowers. It migrates along the Pacific coast in March and April. Later, from July through September, when the blooming season at higher elevations is at its peak, the Calliope uses the mountain ranges as breeding grounds and as a southward migration route.

Description Its size and the male's elegant gorget help identify the Calliope, the smallest of North American hummingbirds. The male's gorget is rose purple interspersed with streaks of white. Aside from the gorget, the male is very much like the female, iridescent green above, cinnamon buff along the sides, and whitish below. The female is difficult to distinguish from the female Allen's or Rufous. In both sexes a relatively short bill and short tail are helpful identification clues. Size: 2⅘ to 3½ inches.

Habitat Showing no particular preference for either conifers or broad-leaved trees, the Calliope nests at the edges of mountain streams and adjacent to glades and meadows.

Calliope Hummingbird (*Stellula calliope*)

Costa's Hummingbird (*Calypte costae*)

During migration, the birds appear in a wider range of habitats, including irrigated lands and gardens.

Nesting The female often builds her nest on top of the previous year's nest. There are two-, three-, and sometimes four-story nests built by the same bird in different years. The nests, which are constructed of bark, leaves, moss, and fine down from leaves and stems of plants, blend so well into the surroundings that they can be mistaken for a pinecone or a knot on a branch. Snug and well insulated, they are designed to protect the female from cold at high elevations.

The two eggs take about 15 days to hatch and the young leave anywhere from 18 to 23 days after hatching. In defense of his territory and as part of his courtship display, the male rises to a considerable height and makes an aerial dive. He may also make U-shaped flights or hover slowly over an intruder before giving chase.

Favorite nectar plants Both on its nesting grounds and during migration, the Calliope visits a wide range of flowering plants. Favorites

are American columbine (*Aquilegia*), currant (*Ribes*), lousewort (*Pedicularis canadensis*), monkeyflower (*Mimulus*), orange (*Citrus sinensis*), penstemon (*Penstemon*), and sage (*Salvia*).

Costa's Hummingbird

Calypte costae

Range The Costa's makes its home in the Southwest, where it has little competition with other species of hummingbirds. Its breeding range stretches from central California, southern Nevada, and

southwestern Utah southward into Mexico. In the fall there is a partial withdrawal southward and an eastward movement that sees some individuals reaching the Texas and Louisiana coasts. In southern California, where the Costa's is well adapted to urban districts, it is a year-round resident.

Description The bright violet to violet-blue gorget and crown of the male are the best identifying features of this species. The gorget extends outward on each side and reaches downward along the bird's flanks. Under some conditions the gorget and crown may look black, greenish, magenta, or purple. The back is a metallic green, and the undersurface is white with olive green sides. The female, indistinguishable from the female Black-chinned, is green above and whitish below. The bill in both sexes is somewhat shorter than in other species of North American hummingbirds. Size: 3 to 3½ inches.

Habitat The Costa's is less dependent upon water than other North American hummingbirds and is therefore able to withstand desert conditions. It is, however, equally at home in urban districts, having adapted well to irrigation and settlement.

Nesting In some coastal districts of southern California, nesting gets under way as early as December. But in the remainder of the range, the usual time is March or April. The nest is loosely constructed

of plant down and may contain feathers, pieces of paper, and dry leaves. The material is held together with spider silk. In desert habitat the nest is often built in dead yuccas.

The incubation period for the two white eggs is about 16 days, and young leave the nest in 20 to 23 days. Usually only one brood is reared in a season. The male defends an uncommonly large nesting territory from two to four acres—to ensure a sufficient nectar supply. Using dive displays and aggressive chasing, he is usually successful in keeping intruders away. In many cases, the display dive is accompanied by a high, thin whistle.

Favorite nectar plants The Costa's is somewhat limited in its choice of flowers. Its bill is too short to probe flowers with very long floral tubes. Among the flowers that it successfully visits for nectar are lemon bottlebrush (*Callistemon citrinus*), chuparosa (*Justicia californica*), coralbells (*Heuchera sanguinea*), Mexican sage (*Salvia leucantha*), ocotillo (*Fouquieria splendens*), scarlet larkspur (*Delphinium cardinale*), and tree tobacco (*Nicotiana glauca*).

Magnificent Hummingbird (*Eugenes fulgens*)

Ruby-throated Hummingbird (*Archilochus colubris*)

Magnificent (Rivoli) Hummingbird

Eugenes fulgens

Range The Magnificent can be found in many of the mountain canyons of Arizona and New Mexico. It has also ventured into southern Colorado. Except for a few that stay

behind each year in southern Arizona, the entire population migrates to Mexico for the winter.

Description Its large size, dark coloration, and long bill help distinguish the Magnificent from smaller species. The male has a bright green gorget, which contrasts sharply with his black underparts. His crown is an iridescent purple and his back, bronze green. The female is green above and grayish below, with light spotting on the throat. Size: 4½ to 5 inches.

Habitat During the breeding season the Magnificent is found chiefly in mountain canyons at elevations between 5,000 and 8,500 feet. In seeking nectar, the birds frequent open areas where wildflowers are present.

Nesting Although the Magnificent returns to its northern breeding range in the Southwest as early as March, nesting rarely gets under way until sometime in May. By July the nesting season is all but over, but the birds may still be present until October and later. The nest is usually high up on the horizontal limb of a pine, oak, maple, sycamore, or Douglas fir. The nest is largely composed of soft plant material and feathers and is saddled to a limb with spider webbing. The outside is covered with lichens.

Favorite nectar plants Century plant (*Agave americana*) is especially popular with the Magnificent, but it frequently visits other flowers, including columbine (*Aquilegia*), desert honeysuckle (*Anisacanthus thurberi*), geranium (*Geranium*), Huachuca agave (*Agave parryi*), iris (*Iris*), penstemon (*Penstemon*), scarlet sage (*Salvia splendens*), and trumpet honeysuckle (*Lonicera sempervirens*).

Ruby-throated Hummingbird

Archilochus colubris

Range The Ruby-throated is the only hummingbird that nests east of the Mississippi, and the only one that regularly migrates across the Gulf of Mexico. Its breeding range extends as far west as Alberta,

east to Nova Scotia, and southward through the eastern United States to the Gulf Coast and south-central Texas. The Ruby-throated migrates to its winter range in southern Mexico to Panama either by crossing the Gulf of Mexico or making its way by land through eastern Texas and eastern Mexico. (The more westerly nesting Ruby-throated take the land route.) A few spend the winter in southern Florida and along the Gulf Coast.

Migration northward begins as early as late February, but the birds do not begin to reach the more northern portions of the breeding range until May. The return flight extends from late July until late October.

Description Both the male and female Ruby-throated are an iridescent green above and are largely white below. The male has a bright ruby gorget and olive-tinged sides. The gorget may look golden or greenish if viewed in side light, black in very poor light. A small white spot is discernible just behind the eye in both sexes. Size: 3 to 3¾ inches.

Habitat This species commonly nests in open woodlands, parks, and gardens where its favorite flowers are in good supply. Occasionally it nests in parkland in urban districts. The nesting population often increases where hummingbird feeders are in constant supply.

Nesting The nest is constructed of downy plant material, bud scales, and leaves, with lichens on the outside surface. It is firmly anchored to the top of a horizontal limb with spider webbing. Trees commonly chosen for nest sites include pines, oaks, hickories, hornbeams, and tulippoplars.

Rufous Hummingbird (*Selasphorus rufus*)

The two eggs are incubated for about 16 days. Fledging periods are generally 20 or 21 days. One or two broods are reared in a season.

As part of his courtship behavior, the male rises to about 10 or 15 feet, then dives in a U-shaped arc, coming up again to about the same height. At the bottom of the dive, he makes a loud buzzing noise with his wings and tail. In a display associated with territorial defense, the male flies back and forth in front of an intruder.

Favorite nectar plants
Among the plants that have the greatest appeal are beebalm (*Monarda didyma*), American columbine (*Aquilegia canadensis*), jewelweed (*Impatiens capensis*), gladiolus (*Gladiolus*), Japanese honeysuckle (*Lonicera japonica*), nasturtium (*Tropaeolum majus*), red buckeye (*Aesculus pavia*), silk tree or mimosa (*Albizia julibrissin*), trumpet creeper (*Campsis radicans*), and trumpet honeysuckle (*Lonicera sempervirens*). In spring before many flowers are in bloom, the Ruby-throated feeds on sap flowing from holes made in trees by woodpeckers.

Rufous Hummingbird

Selasphorus rufus

Range The Rufous is the most widely distributed and the most abundant hummingbird in the West. Its breeding range extends from southern Alaska and the southern Yukon Territory, south to Oregon,

and the northern tip of California, and as far east as southwestern Alberta and western Montana. Rufous that nest in the far north undertake a journey of as many as 3,000 miles along the Pacific coast from the southern parts of Mexico where they spend the winter.

The southward migration in the fall is largely by way of the Rocky Mountains, but some Rufous may wander off course and appear along the Texas and Louisiana coasts.

Both the spring and fall flights extend over a long period of time because some birds leave earlier than others. The northerly migration flight

takes from February to May, and the flight southward from late June until October. When migrating, the Rufous flies for long periods then stops for as long as a week or more at favorable locations where food is plentiful.

Description The dominant orange-red of the male, which extends from the head to the back and tail, helps distinguish this species from its close relatives the Broad-tailed and Allen's, though the Rufous too may have an iridescent green back. The gorget is an iridescent orange-red in good light but may seem golden-green under some light conditions. The female Rufous is mostly green above and white below. Adult females show speckles of orange-red on the throat. Size: 3⅓ to 4 inches.

Habitat During migration the Rufous visits a wide variety of habitats, including orchards and gardens. The typical nesting habitat is woodland that is dominated by conifers and has openings where wildflowers grow. The nest site may be close to a human habitation.

Nesting In the more southern parts of the breeding range, nesting gets under way

in April. Farther north, nesting generally doesn't begin until July. The nest is constructed of moss, willow down, and rootlets and is held together with spiderwebs. The lichens that cover the outside serve as camouflage. The two eggs are incubated for about 12 days, and young, often too large for the nest, leave in about 20 days.

The males guard not only their nesting territories but also the feeding territories they establish during pauses between migrational flights. Their displays consist of a series of oval-shaped dives with a loud buzz heard on the downswing, followed by a whining note, and then a rattle.

Favorite nectar plants
One of the flowers most eagerly sought is the shrubby red-flowering currant (*Ribes sanguineum*). Other frequently visited flowers include abutilon (*Abutilon*), beebalm (*Monarda didyma*), cape-honeysuckle (*Tecomaria capensis*), columbine (*Aquilegia*), fuchsia (*Fuchsia*), larkspur (*Delphinium*), lupine (*Lupinus*), paintbrush (*Castilleja*), and penstemon (*Penstemon*).

Pipe Vine Swallowtail (*Battus philenor*)

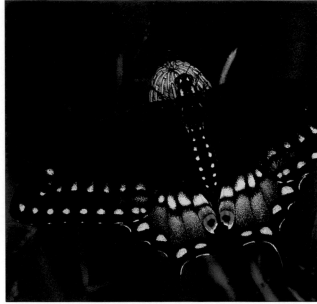

Black Swallowtail (*Papilio polyxenes*)

FAMILY PAPILIONIDAE: SWALLOWTAILS

Pipe Vine Swallowtail

Battus philenor

Range and background
This large black-and-purple swallowtail is found throughout most of the United States, but especially in the southern Appalachian Mountains. The spread of the pipe vine plant

as a gardening favorite has resulted in a similar spread of this butterfly, which uses pipe vine almost exclusively as its larval host plant. The Pipe Vine Swallowtail can be found on the wing almost throughout the year in the South, and from spring to fall in the cooler areas of the North. This butterfly's relation with five other butterflies—the similarly patterned Tiger, Black, and Spicebush swallowtails,

and the Red-spotted Purple and female Diana—is a great example of "mimicry." All of the latter avoid predation by mimicking the color and flight behavior of the Pipe Vine Swallowtail, which absorbs chemicals from its host plant that are distasteful to birds and other predators.

Description   This swallowtail is unique in that it is mostly black above with a bluish iridescence on the hind wing; it also has a row of orange spots along the margin of the ventral hind wing. Size: 2¾ to 4½ inches.

Habitat   The Pipe Vine Swallowtail is often found in open forests where its host plant grows naturally, but it also flourishes in meadows, parks, and gardens, and on roadsides.

Habits   The wings of the Pipe Vine Swallowtail flutter quickly while the butterfly takes nectar. Males of this species patrol in search of females during the warm hours of the day.

Larval host and larvae
Larvae feed on various species of pipe vine (*Aristolochia*). Larvae are black or brown with red tubercles (small, knobby projections) along each side of their back.

Favorite nectar plants
Butterfly bush (*Buddleia davidii*), lilac (*Syringa*), azalea (*Rhododendron*), petunia (*Petunia*).

Black Swallowtail

Papilio polyxenes

Range and background
This swallowtail is common through most of the United States, except in the extreme West. It can also be found in southeastern Canada. The Black Swallowtail's favorite

host plants are members of the carrot family, so this species is a frequent visitor to

many home vegetable gardens. The Black Swallowtail is usually on the wing from spring to fall, but may be seen for a slightly longer period in warm areas. To avoid predators, the female mimics the Pipe Vine Swallowtail in color and movement.

Description   The Black Swallowtail is mostly black with patches of yellow. The male has a narrow yellow band on both wings; the female has a series of small yellow spots. Size: 2½ to 3½ inches.

Habitat   This butterfly may be seen in many types of open spaces, including gardens, meadows, and roadsides.

Habits   The Black Swallowtail has a more lilting flight than the Pipe Vine Swallowtail, but it also flutters its wings when taking nectar. During cool periods, members of this species can be found basking close to the ground with their wings spread (dorsal basking).

Larval host and larvae
Larvae feed on various members of the carrot family,

Anise Swallowtail (*Papilio zelicaon*)

Giant Swallowtail (*Papilio cresphontes*)

including carrot, parsley, celery, and dill. Young larvae are black with white markings, resembling bird droppings. Mature larvae are green with black bands that have yellow or orange spots.

Favorite nectar plants
Butterfly weed (*Asclepias tuberosa*), phlox (*Phlox*), clover (*Trifolium*), thistle (*Cirsium*).

Anise Swallowtail

Papilio zelicaon

Range and background
This brilliantly colored swallowtail ranges throughout the western United States and southwestern Canada. It can be seen flitting through canyons and meadows where its

favorite host plant, fennel (or wild anise), grows. The Anise Swallowtail is on the wing throughout the year in southern California, and in May and

June in the remainder of its range. This butterfly is especially at home in southern California, where fennel abounds on roadsides, in vacant lots, in mountain canyons, and in gardens. Because fennel is easy to grow and store, the Anise Swallowtail can be raised from egg to adult indoors in a netted cage, then let go.

Descripton The Anise Swallowtail is yellow and black, with patches of blue on the hind wings and an orange spot on the inside of each hind wing. Size: 2⅝ to 3⅛ inches.

Habitat This species is found in a wide range of habitats, from mountain peaks to lowland valleys. In urban areas, it is often seen in vacant lots, canyons, parks, and gardens.

Habits Males spend their time on hilltops, where they perch and patrol in search of females. They also form mud-puddle clubs, congregating around and taking moisture from wet areas.

Larval host and larvae
Larvae feed on various members of the carrot family, including carrot, parsley, fennel, and anise. Young larvae are black with white markings, resembling bird droppings. Mature larvae are green with black bands that have yellow spots.

Favorite nectar plants
Lantana (*Lantana*), zinnia (*Zinnia*), butterfly bush (*Buddleia davidii*), lily-of-the-Nile (*Agapanthus*).

Giant Swallowtail

Papilio cresphontes

Range and background The Giant Swallowtail can be found throughout most of the United States, but is especially common in the South. It can be seen throughout the year in

warmer areas and from spring to fall in cooler regions. It has the distinction of being known

as much for its larvae (called orange dogs) as for the adult butterflies, because the larvae have been notorious pests on citrus crops, especially orange trees. This notoriety is useful information for butterfly gardeners; they can simply plant a few orange trees to attract this lovely butterfly to their garden.

Description The Giant Swallowtail is black above, with patches of yellow. It is mostly yellow below, with black veins and margins. Size: 3⅜ to 5½ inches.

Habitat This species frequents various open areas, including parks, gardens, and orchards.

Habits A long, high, lilting flight pattern characterizes the Giant Swallowtail. As with other swallowtails, males patrol in search of receptive females. Males will also visit mud or sand, taking moisture from these wet areas.

Larval host and larvae
Various types of citrus trees, especially orange trees, are

Tiger Swallowtail (*Papilio glaucus*)

Spicebush Swallowtail (*Papilio troilus*)

the principal host plants. Larvae are brown with mottled white patches, especially on the rear end.

Favorite nectar plants
Honeysuckle (*Lonicera*), azalea (*Rhododendron*), goldenrod (*Solidago*), orange trees (*Citrus sinensis*).

Tiger Swallowtail

Papilio glaucus

Range and background
This swallowtail is common throughout the eastern United States and Canada. It is usually on the wing from spring to fall and sometimes longer in warm areas. Like some of the

other swallowtails, the female Tiger Swallowtail has evolved a dark form that mimics the Pipe Vine Swallowtail and

thereby escapes predation. Like the Giant Swallowtail, the Tiger Swallowtail is one of the largest North American butterflies. The closely related Western Tiger Swallowtail (*Papilio rutulus*) ranges throughout the western United States, feeding on some of the same types of flowers as its eastern relative and exhibiting many of the same habits.

Description The Tiger Swallowtail is mostly yellow above and below, with black bands and margins; its ventral hind wings have blue patches and orange spots along the margin. Size: 3 to 6½ inches.

Habitat This species occurs in woodlands, parks, and gardens.

Habits A high flier, this butterfly often takes nectar on flowering trees, but it will feed from shorter plants as well. Males patrol various areas in search of females.

Larval host and larvae The female selects a variety of trees and shrubs as host plants, including wild cherry (*Prunus*), willow (*Salix*), cottonwood (*Populus*), and tulip-poplar (*Liriodendron tulipifera*). Larvae are green, with a pair of large eyespots on the front part of the thorax.

Favorite nectar plants
Butterfly bush (*Buddleia davidii*), lilac (*Syringa*), honeysuckle (*Lonicera*), butterfly weed (*Asclepias tuberosa*).

Spicebush Swallowtail

Papilio troilus

Range and background
This striking swallowtail, similar in appearance to the Pipe Vine, the female Black, and the dark form of the female Tiger Swallowtail, occurs throughout the eastern United

States and southeastern Canada, wherever its host plants,

sassafras and spicebush, grow. Native to the East, spicebush and sassafras can easily be grown in home gardens throughout the butterfly's range. Although it is a woodland butterfly, the Spicebush Swallowtail finds itself very much at home in gardens.

Description Members of this species are mostly black above, with patches of metallic blue on the hind wing and white spots along the wing margins. Orange spots on the ventral hind wing also distinguish the Spicebush Swallowtail. Size: 3 to 5 inches.

Habitat Woodlands, fields, gardens, and parks provide habitat for this butterfly.

Habits A low flier, the Spicebush Swallowtail can often be seen on a somewhat rapid and direct flight pattern. Males patrol woodland and roadside areas looking for females and often gather at mud puddles.

Larval host and larvae
Larvae feed on spicebush (*Lindera benzoin*) and sassafras (*Sassafras albidum*).

Checkered White (*Pontia protodice*)

European Cabbage Butterfly (*Pieris rapae*)

Clouded Sulfur (*Colias philodice*)

Larvae are similar to those of the Tiger Swallowtail, except that they have two pairs of eyespots on the front part of the thorax.

Favorite nectar plants Honeysuckle (*Lonicera*), lantana (*Lantana*), azalea (*Rhododendron*), butterfly weed (*Asclepias tuberosa*).

FAMILY PIERIDAE: WHITES AND SULFURS

Checkered White

Pontia protodice

Range and background
This black-and-white butterfly can be seen throughout much of the United States and southern Canada, excluding the Pacific Northwest. It is generally on the wing from

spring to fall, and the year around in warm areas. The Checkered White frequents open spaces and often visits home gardens. Its larvae feed

on certain members of the mustard family, such as cabbage, turnip, and mustard, so it is attracted to both vegetable and flower gardens.

Description The Checkered White is mostly white above, with black patches that generally form a checkered pattern. Size: 1½ to 2 inches.

Habitat This butterfly inhabits a wide range of usually dry, open areas, including agricultural land, vacant lots, and roadsides, as well as gardens.

Habits The Checkered White has a darting flight. Males patrol in search of females. Sometimes great numbers of this butterfly are seen together.

Larval host and larvae Larvae feed on various members of the mustard family, including mustard, turnip, and cabbage. Beeplant (*Cleome*) is also a larval host. Larvae are greenish, with yellow and gray stripes.

Favorite nectar plants Aster (*Aster*), butterfly weed (*Asclepias tuberosa*), centaury (*Centaurium*).

European Cabbage Butterfly

Pieris rapae

Range and background
Well known to anyone who observes butterflies, the European Cabbage Butterfly, as the name implies, was introduced to North America (in Quebec in 1860). It has since become

perhaps the most widespread and common species in North America. It was also introduced to Hawaii and has become established there as well. The European Cabbage Butterfly is on the wing throughout the year in warm areas and from spring to fall farther north.

Description Members of this species are mostly white above, with black-tipped forewings. Males have one black spot in the middle of the forewing, females have two. Size: 1½ to 2 inches.

Habitat This species occupies gardens, agricultural lands, vacant lots, and other open areas.

Habits Males patrol in search of females and engage in mud-puddling.

Larval host and larvae Larvae of this species feed on a wide range of plants in the mustard family. They favor such cultivated vegetables as cabbage, cauliflower, broccoli, and radish, as well as nasturtium (*Tropaeolum majus*). Larvae are light green, with a thin yellow line on the back and sides.

Favorite nectar plants A wide range of garden flowers, including lantana (*Lantana*), impatiens (*Impatiens*), marigold (*Tagetes*), mint (*Mentha*), and dandelion (*Taraxacum*).

Clouded Sulfur

Colias philodice

Range and background
This dainty yellow butterfly is common throughout most of North America, except for Florida, Texas, and coastal California. It is on the wing from spring to late fall in most

Cloudless Sulfur (*Phoebis sennae*)

Sleepy Orange (*Eurema nicippe*)

areas, sometimes longer in warm areas. It is also known as the Mud Puddle Butterfly, because males are fond of gathering around moist areas on roadsides and in gardens. This butterfly, as well as the closely related Orange or Alfalfa Sulfur (*Colias eurytheme*), has followed the spread of agriculture, since the larvae feed on various members of the pea family, such as clover and alfalfa. Although pests to farmers, both species are ideal for butterfly gardeners, since clover and alfalfa are easy to grow in home gardens.

Description   The Clouded Sulfur is mostly yellow above, with black margins, and has a black spot on the forewing. (The Orange Sulfur looks similar, but is more orange than yellow above.) Size: 1⅛ to 2⅜ inches.

Habitat   This butterfly can be found in various open areas where clover abounds, including fields, roadsides, parks, and gardens.

Habits   Members of this species can often be seen basking with their wings closed, sideways to the sun. Males patrol areas looking for females and

often congregate at mud puddles. Sometimes the Clouded and Orange sulfurs interbreed, producing hybrid butterflies that have certain characteristics of both species.

Larval host and larvae
Various members of the pea family, especially clovers (*Trifolium*), are the principal host plants. (The Orange Sulfur is more partial to alfalfa.) Larvae are dark green, with a dark stripe on the back and a lighter stripe on the side.

Favorite nectar plants
Aster (*Aster*), goldenrod (*Solidago*), phlox (*Phlox*), clover (*Trifolium*).

Cloudless Sulfur

Phoebis sennae

Range and background
Common throughout the southern United States, this large yellow butterfly is on the wing the year around in the South. It regularly appears as an immigrant farther north during the summer. In the fall, it often embarks on mass

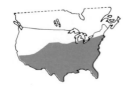

emigrations, usually in a southeasterly direction because it cannot survive northern winters. Its species name is derived from its host plant name, senna.

Description   Males are yellow above; females may be yellow or yellow-orange or whitish. Size: 2⅛ to 2¾ inches.

Habitat   The Cloudless Sulfur prefers open, sunny areas, such as parks, gardens, and shorelines.

Habits   Males patrol in search of females and often form mud-puddle congregations. Though usually a somewhat low flier, the Cloudless Sulfur will flutter up into trees to obtain nectar from the flowers there.

Larval host and larvae
Various species of senna (*Cassia*) are selected as host plants. Larvae are yellowish green, with a series of dark bands across the body.

Favorite nectar plants
Lantana (*Lantana*), bougainvillea (*Bougainvillea*), hibiscus (*Hibiscus*), morning glory (*Ipomoea*).

Sleepy Orange

Eurema nicippe

Range and background
This striking orange butterfly is common throughout the southern United States. On the wing the year around in the southern states, the Sleepy Orange also may be seen from

spring to late fall farther north. Sometimes large swarms of Sleepy Oranges are seen on massive emigrations.

Description   Members of this species are mostly a rich orange above, with black margins on the wings, and predominantly yellow below. Size: 1⅜ to 1⅞ inches.

Habitat   Sleepy Orange butterflies are found in various open areas, including parks, gardens, vacant lots, fields, and roadsides.

Habits   Contrary to its name, this butterfly has a darting, erratic flight. Males patrol in search of females and often congregate at mud puddles.

Small Copper (*Lycaena phlaeas*)

Gray Hairstreak (*Strymon melinus*)

Spring Azure (*Celastrina ladon*)

Larval host and larvae
Larvae feed almost exclusively on various species of senna (*Cassia*). Larvae are green, with a white, black-bordered stripe on the side.

Favorite nectar plants
Composites, such as shepherd's-needle (*Bidens*).

FAMILY LYCAENIDAE: GOSSAMER WINGS

Small (American) Copper

Lycaena phlaeas

Range and background
Common throughout the northeastern United States and eastern Canada, the Small Copper is also found as far south as Arkansas and Georgia and locally in western mountains. It can be seen on the

wing from spring to fall. This species has become adapted to disturbed habitats, where its

host plants sorrel and dock (both introduced from Europe) grow. This butterfly's bright colors and small size make it easy to recognize and identify.

Description The Small Copper is bright copper above, with grayish black margins. It is mostly gray below with an orange band near the margin of the hind wing. Size: ⅞ to 1¼ inches.

Habitat This butterfly is found in all sorts of disturbed areas, including vacant lots, landfills, fields, and gardens.

Habits Males perch on grasses or tall flowers and can be seen interacting with almost any passing insect.

Larval host and larvae
Larvae in the eastern range of this species feed on sheep sorrel (*Rumex acetosella*) and curled dock (*Rumex crispus*). Western mountain populations select mountain sorrel (*Oxyria digyna*). Larvae range in color from rose red to green.

Favorite nectar plants
Butterfly weed (*Asclepias tuberosa*), goldenrod (*Solidago*), yarrow (*Achillea*), buttercup (*Ranunculus*).

Gray Hairstreak

Strymon melinus

Range and background The Gray Hairstreak is common throughout the United States and southern Canada. It can be seen on the wing from spring to fall in most areas. It is distinctive in that its larvae

feed on a wide variety of host plants, from common garden hibiscus to beans. It can be a pest on cotton, hops, and bean crops.

Description The Gray Hairstreak is dark gray above and light gray below, with orange spots on the bottom tip of the hind wing. Size: ⅞ to 1¼ inches.

Habitat This butterfly thrives in a wide variety of habitats, including parks, gardens, vacant lots, and open fields.

Habit The Gray Hairstreak is commonly seen perched on plants and rubbing its hind wings back and forth (as many hairstreaks do). Males

often perch in the same spot on a shrub or tree for the afternoon, flying swiftly to and from this spot from time to time.

Larval host and larvae The larvae feed on a wide variety of host plants, including hibiscus (*Hibiscus*), clover (*Trifolium*), mallow (*Malva*), beans (*Phaseolus*), and vetch (*Vicia*). Larvae range in color from reddish brown to green.

Favorite nectar plants
Goldenrod (*Solidago*), milkweed (*Asclepias*), clover (*Trifolium*), winter cress (*Barbarea*).

Spring Azure

Celastrina ladon

Range and background
This species is widespread throughout North America. It is on the wing from early spring to fall, and sometimes longer in the Deep South. The Spring Azure is one of the

earliest butterflies to emerge from its pupa and thus heralds

Gulf Fritillary (*Agraulis vanillae*)

Great Spangled Fritillary (*Speyeria cybele*)

Variegated Fritillary (*Euptoieta claudia*)

the beginning of spring
and the good weather
to come.

Description   The Spring
Azure is generally metallic-
blue above and gray below,
but exhibits large variations
in color depending on the season and the geographic region
where it is found. Size: ¾ to
1¼ inches.

Habitat   This species
frequents woodlands, parks,
open glades, fields, and
roadsides.

Habits   Females often fly up
into trees, such as dogwood,
and deposit eggs on the flower
buds. Males can be seen congregating in mud-puddle clubs
on moist soil alongside streams
or roads.

Larval host and larvae
Selected host plants include
various shrubs and trees: dogwood (*Cornus*), viburnum
(*Viburnum*), New-Jersey-tea
(*Ceanothus*), blueberry
(*Vaccinium*). Larvae are
greenish or pinkish, with a
dark stripe on the back.

Favorite nectar plants
Rockcress (*Arabis*), buckeye
(*Aesculus*), violet (*Viola*),
winter cress (*Barbarea*), dandelion (*Taraxacum*).

FAMILY NYMPHALIDAE: BRUSH-FOOTED BUTTERFLIES

Gulf Fritillary

Agraulis vanillae

Range and background
This primarily tropical species
extends its range temporarily
each summer into some of the
states in the north. It is now
established in parts of California and Hawaii. It is on the

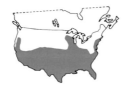

wing throughout the year in
the Deep South, and from
spring to fall farther north. It
is characterized by its distinctive long wings and their
contrasting upper and lower
patterns. Gulf Fritillary larvae
can be reared in captivity, and
the butterfly itself is easy to
attract since its host plant is
in common garden use in
many parts of the butterfly's
range.

Description   The Gulf Fritillary is orange above, with
parallel black lines running

vertically on the wings. Its
underside is mostly brownish,
with numerous silver spots.
Size: 2 to 3 inches.

Habitat   This species can be
found in gardens, parks, fields,
and other open areas.

Habits   Sometimes mass
emigrations of this butterfly
occur throughout its range.
The Gulf Fritillary is a
rapid flier.

Larval host and larvae
Various species of passion vine
(*Passiflora*) are the principal
host plants. The larvae are
mostly black, with red stripes
and numerous black spines
running down the body.

Favorite nectar plants
Lantana (*Lantana*), impatiens
(*Impatiens*), shepherd's-
needle (*Bidens*), thistle
(*Cirsium*).

Variegated Fritillary

Euptoieta claudia

Range and background
This tawny butterfly is common throughout the South,
and it extends its range into
most northern states during

the summer. The Variegated
Fritillary is generally on the

wing from early spring to late
fall, sometimes longer in the
Deep South. This butterfly
cannot survive the northern
winters, however, and thus
the emigrants die each year.

Description   Members of
this species are mostly dark
orange above, with numerous
black lines throughout. Size:
1¾ to 2½ inches.

Habitat   The Variegated
Fritillary frequents a variety
of open areas, including fields,
roadsides, and meadows.

Habits   This butterfly is a
fast flier, usually along a low
plane. Males patrol areas in
search of females.

Larval host and larvae   A
wide range of host plants,
including violets (*Viola*), passion vine (*Passiflora*), and
stonecrop (*Sedum*) are selected as host plants. Larvae
are mostly orange, with black
stripes and numerous black
spines running down the body.

Pearl Crescent (*Phyciodes tharos*)

American Painted Lady (*Vanessa virginiensis*)

Favorite nectar plants
Butterfly weed (*Asclepias tuberosa*), clover (*Trifolium*), shepherd's-needle (*Bidens*), milkweed (*Asclepias*).

Great Spangled Fritillary

Speyeria cybele

Range and background
This species is found throughout the United States, except for the extreme South. Unlike

many other species, there is only one generation each year of the Great Spangled Fritillary. This species is on the wing from late spring or early summer to fall.

Description   The Great Spangled Fritillary is among the larger fritillaries. It is mostly orange above, with small black patches and lines. It is also mostly orange below, with the silver spots common to fritillaries. Size: 2⅛ to 3¾ inches.

Habitat   This butterfly is mostly found in moist areas,

such as meadows, woods, and stream sides and other open spaces.

Habits   A fast flier, the Great Spangled Fritillary is a visitor of thistle and milkweed flowers. Males patrol in search of females.

Larval host and larvae
Larvae feed on various species of violet (*Viola*). They are black, with numerous black spines running down the body.

Favorite nectar plants
Gloriosa daisy (*Rudbeckia hirta*), thistle (*Cirsium*), verbena (*Verbena*), butterfly weed (*Asclepias tuberosa*).

Pearl Crescent

Phyciodes tharos

Range and background   The Pearl Crescent is common throughout most of the United States, except the Northwest and extreme Southwest. It is usually on the wing from spring to fall and can be seen

the year around in areas of the far South. One of the

most ubiquitous of the summer fliers, this species is known to dart out after objects large and small.

Description   This butterfly is predominantly orange above, with numerous black patches and a black margin. It is mostly a lighter orange below. Size: 1 to 1¼ inches.

Habitat   The Pearl Crescent can be found in various open areas where its host plant, aster, occurs, including vacant lots, fields, roadsides, and meadows.

Habits   Males are active mud-puddlers and are often seen patrolling open areas in search of females. The Pearl Crescent is a dorsal basker and a low flier.

Larval host and larvae   The larvae feed on various species of aster (*Aster*). They are mostly black, with yellow bands and spots, and numerous black spines running down the body.

Favorite nectar plants
Composites, such as thistle (*Cirsium*), aster (*Aster*), gloriosa daisy (*Rudbeckia hirta*).

American Painted Lady

Vanessa virginiensis

Range and background
Although widespread throughout the United States (including Hawaii but not Alaska), this butterfly is more commonly seen in the East than in the West. It is on the wing

from spring to fall and can be seen the year around in some regions of the far South. Like the closely related Painted Lady, its numbers fluctuate from one year to the next. With its exquisitely, brightly colored upper side and many-patterned underside, this butterfly is truly a sight to see.

Description   The American Painted Lady is mostly orange above, with black-and-white wing tips and blue spots on the hind wings. It is variously patterned below, with two large eyespots on the hind wings. Size: 1¾ to 2¼ inches.

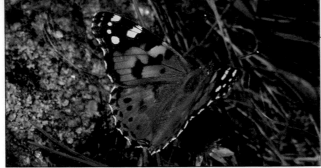
Painted Lady (*Vanessa cardui*)

Buckeye (*Junonia coenia*)

Monarch (*Danaus plexippus*)

Habitat The American Painted Lady favors open, sunny areas, including gardens, parks, stream sides, and vacant lots.

Habits Males perch and wait for females to pass by. They also gather at wet areas to take moisture. Unlike its cousin, the Painted Lady, this butterfly is only occasionally migratory.

Larval host and larvae The larvae feed on various types of everlasting (*Gnaphalium, Anaphalis, Antennaria*). They are mostly black with yellow cross bands and a row of white spots on each side.

Favorite nectar plants Marigold (*Tagetes*), goldenrod (*Solidago*), aster (*Aster*), butterfly bush (*Buddleia davidii*).

Painted Lady (Cosmopolitan)

Vanessa cardui

Range and background The Painted Lady occurs throughout North America, including Hawaii and southernmost Alaska, but is more likely to be seen in the northern United States and southern Canada.

This species, however, is not a permanent resident in the United States and Canada; it generally recolonizes from northern Mexico following the onset of spring. Also known as the Cosmopolitan, it ranges throughout the world because of its migratory habits. Sometimes the emigrations reach great numbers. Emigrating individuals of this species rarely survive northern winters but under favorable conditions, new individuals will recolonize from Mexico the following spring.

Description The Painted Lady is mostly orange above, with black-and-white wing tips and black spots on the hind wings. It is many-patterned below, with a row of small eyespots on the hind wings. Size: 2 to 2½ inches.

Habitat This species frequents a wide range of habitats, including gardens, parks, meadows, deserts, and vacant lots.

Habits Sometimes mass emigrations of the Painted Lady can be seen flying low to the ground. Males usually perch and wait for females to venture by, but they sometimes patrol for them as well.

Larval host and larvae Larvae feed on a wide variety of host plants, but especially thistle (*Cirsium*). They also feed on mallow (*Malva*) and hollyhock (*Alcea*). Larvae are greenish, mottled with black, and have dark hairy spines running down the body.

Favorite nectar plants Aster (*Aster*), cosmos (*Cosmos*), thistle (*Cirsium*), buttonbush (*Cephalanthus*).

Buckeye

Junonia coenia

Range and background This distinctive butterfly is well known for the large eyespots on its upper side. The Buckeye is primarily a southern species although it emigrates north in the summer. It

cannot withstand northern winters, however, so is a resident only in the southern part of its range. On the eastern seaboard, large masses of emigrating Buckeyes can sometimes be seen.

Description The Buckeye is mostly brown above, with a series of large eyespots: one on each forewing and two on each hind wing. Size: 1⅝ to 2½ inches.

Habitat The Buckeye can be found in a wide variety of open spaces, including fields, trails, roadsides, and shorelines.

Habits Fond of basking on bare ground, this butterfly will return again and again to the same spot. It has a rapid, darting flight. Males visit mud puddles for moisture.

Larval host and larvae Favored larval hosts include plantain (*Plantago*), snapdragon (*Antirrhinum*), and toadflax (*Linaria*). Larvae are mostly blackish, with blue-black spines running down the body.

Silver-spotted Skipper (*Epargyreus clarus*)

Checkered Skipper (*Pyrgus communis*)

Favorite nectar plants
Aster (*Aster*), coreopsis
(*Coreopsis*), knapweed (*Centaurea*), chicory (*Cichorium*).

Monarch

Danaus plexippus

Range and background
Widespread throughout Canada and the United States, including Hawaii and the southernmost regions of Alaska, the Monarch is perhaps the best-known butterfly

in North America. It may be seen from spring to fall (the year around in warm areas) wherever its milkweed host plant is growing. The Monarch is the only truly migratory butterfly; eastern and midwestern individuals overwinter in the fir forests of central Mexico, and far western individuals travel to the California coast for the winter. There they perch on pine and eucalyptus trees and occasionally go forth to forage for nectar, especially on warm

days. The Monarch has a well-known kinship with the Viceroy butterfly. The latter closely resembles the unpalatable Monarch and thereby tricks birds into ignoring it.

Description This large butterfly is orange, with black veins and borders. Males have a small black scent patch on each hind wing. Size: 3½ to 4 inches.

Habitat The Monarch prefers open fields, meadows, and roadsides where milkweeds abound, but is often found flitting through parks and gardens in populated areas.

Habits This butterfly has a soft, lilting flight. Overwintering congregations often cover entire branches of trees.

Larval host and larvae
Larvae feed on various species of milkweed (*Asclepias*) and other plants in the milkweed family. They have yellow, black, and white stripes and a pair of black, hairlike appendages on the front and rear.

Favorite nectar plants
Various species of milkweed (*Asclepias*), lantana (*Lantana*), lilac (*Syringa*), cosmos (*Cosmos*), goldenrod (*Solidago*), and zinnia (*Zinnia*).

FAMILY HESPERIIDAE: SKIPPERS

Silver-spotted Skipper

Epargyreus clarus

Range and background A common sight in parks and gardens, the Silver-spotted Skipper adapts easily to suburban environments. It is on the

wing from spring to fall in the North and almost the year around in the far South. The silver patch on the ventral hind wing that distinguishes this species can often be seen while the butterfly is in flight.

Description The Silver-spotted Skipper is mostly brown above and below, with a distinctive silver patch on the ventral hind wing. Size: 1¾ to 2½ inches.

Habitat This species can be found in various open and disturbed areas, including gardens, parks, fields, and canyons.

Habits Males usually perch and wait for females to pass by. They will also chase out after other insects from time to time.

Larval host and larvae
Larvae feed primarily on various species of locust (*Robinia*), but they also feed on numerous other legumes. They are yellowish with a reddish head.

Favorite nectar plants
Zinnia (*Zinnia*), honeysuckle (*Lonicera*), butterfly weed (*Asclepias tuberosa*), joe-pye-weed (*Eupatorium*).

Checkered Skipper

Pyrgus communis

Range and background
This black-and-white butterfly is widespread across the United States and southern Canada. It is on the wing the year around in the Deep South

and from spring to fall farther north. It is a frequent garden visitor.

Fiery Skipper (*Hylephila phyleus*)

Sachem (*Atalopedes campestris*)

Description   True to its name, this species is checkered black and white. Size: ¾ to 1¼ inches.

Habitat   The Checkered Skipper can be found in a wide variety of open areas, including gardens, parks, roadsides, and fields.

Habits   This butterfly is a fast flier and usually takes many short flights rather than long ones. Males patrol in search of females and often dart out aggressively toward other butterflies and insects.

Larval host and larvae
Various members of the mallow family, including mallow (*Malva*) and hollyhock (*Alcea*) are the favored host plants. Larvae are yellowish to brownish, with a black head and small white hairs running down the body.

Favorite nectar plants
Aster (*Aster*), fleabane (*Erigeron*), knapweed (*Centaurea*), shepherd's-needle (*Bidens*).

Fiery Skipper

Hylephila phyleus

Range and background
This pretty, small butterfly is familiar to gardeners throughout the southern United States and can be found in Hawaii as well. It is a resident in the

South and emigrates northward in the spring and summer. It is on the wing the year around in the southern portion of its range, and from spring to fall farther north. Since this butterfly selects various grasses as host plants, it is a common garden visitor.

Description   The male is mostly yellow-orange above, with streaks and patches of brown. It is also yellow-orange below, with a number of small, dark spots. The female is darker overall. The Fiery Skipper is also distinguished by its very short antennae. Size: 1 to 1¼ inches.

Habitat   The Fiery Skipper can be found in gardens, parks, fields, and grassland.

Habits   This butterfly darts around from flower to flower in a zigzag pattern, often stopping to perch on the lawn. The fluttering of its wings as it zips by is audible if the listener is close by.

Larval host and larvae
Larvae feed on various grasses, including Bermuda grass (*Cynodon*) and crabgrass (*Digitaria*). They are brownish, with a black head and three dark stripes running down the body.

Favorite nectar plants
Statice (*Limonium*), aster (*Aster*), lantana (*Lantana*), marigold (*Tagetes*), ironweed (*Vernonia*).

Sachem

Atalopedes campestris

Range and background   The Sachem is a resident throughout the southern United States and is on the wing most of the year there. Farther north, where it emigrates each year, it can be seen from spring to

fall. Like the Fiery Skipper, the Sachem uses various grasses as its host plants, so it's a common sight for gardeners across its range.

Description   This butterfly is mostly brownish orange above and below. Males have a large black patch on the dorsal forewing. Size: 1 to 1⅜ inches.

Habitat   This species is found in various disturbed areas, including gardens, parks, fields, and roadsides.

Habits   The Sachem male spends most of the daylight hours perching near to or on the ground. Larvae build a tent at the base of a clump of grass, from which they venture forth to obtain food and to which they return to eat.

Larval host and larvae
Larvae feed on various grasses, including Bermuda grass (*Cynodon*) and crabgrass (*Digitaria*). They are dark green, with a black head and short black hairs running down the body.

Favorite nectar plants
Marigold (*Tagetes*), aster (*Aster*), butterfly weed (*Asclepias tuberosa*), buttonbush (*Cephalanthus*).

Mail-Order Sources

If you can't find the hummingbird and butterfly plants and products you need locally, you may want to contact one of the following sources. This list is by no means complete, but it will give you a place to start. Catalog policies vary; contact each company for current policy and prices.

Arboretum
University of California at Santa Cruz
High and Bay Streets
Santa Cruz, CA 95060
Offers hummingbird plants and information.

Audubon Bookstore
7377 Santa Monica Boulevard
West Hollywood, CA 90046
Features books on hummingbirds, butterflies, and natural history.

Audubon Workshop, Inc.
1501 Paddock Drive
Northbrook, IL 60062
Catalog offers a variety of bird products.

Back Yard Birds and Company
717 South Broadview
Springfield, MO 65809
Books, bird products, and hummingbird feeders are available.

The Brown Company
Yawgoo Pond Road
West Kingston, RI 02892
800-556-7670
National wholesaler distributes nature products including hummingbird feeders, field guides, recordings, and butterfly hibernation boxes.

The Crow's Nest Bookshop
The Laboratory of Ornithology at Cornell University
159 Sapsucker Woods Road
Ithaca, NY 14850
Sells a variety of bird books and products.

Droll Yankees, Inc.
27 Mill Road
Foster, RI 02825
Makes and sells bird feeders and other nature products.

Duncraft
33 Fisherville Road
Penacook, NH 03303
Manufactures and sells hummingbird feeders.

Hyde Bird Feeder Company
56 Felton Street
Box 168
Waltham, MA 02254
Offers hummingbird feeders, books, and other products.

Wild Bird Center
826 Pearl Street
Boulder, CO 80302
Books and hummingbird feeders are available by mail.

For further information on hummingbirds and butterflies, contact the following.

Bird Watcher's Digest
Box 110
149 Acme Street
Marietta, OH 45750
614-373-5285
800-879-2473
Subscription magazine specializes in birds and bird-related activities.

The Lepidopterists' Society
257 Common Street
Dedham, MA 02026-4020
617-326-2634
Membership in this organization is open to anyone interested in lepidoptera.

National Wildflower Research Center
2600 FM 973 North
Austin, TX 78725
512-929-3600
Wildflower conservation organization is a national resource center for information on wildflowers.

National Wildlife Federation
1400 Sixteenth Street NW
Washington DC 20036-2266
202-797-6800
Sponsors Back Yard Wildlife Habitat Program.

Xerces Society
10 Southwest Ash Street
Portland, OR 97204
503-222-2788
Membership organization dedicated to the conservation of invertebrates.

Books for Further Reading

Dennis, John V. A Guide to Western Bird Feeding. Baltimore: Bird Watcher's Digest, 1991.

Dennis, John V. The Wildlife Gardener. New York: Alfred A. Knopf, Inc., 1985.

Howe, William. The Butterflies of North America. Garden City, N.Y.: Doubleday and Company, Inc., 1975.

Johnsgard, Paul A. The Hummingbirds of North America. Washington D.C.: Smithsonian Institution Press, 1983.

Opler, Paul A. and George O. Krizek. Butterflies East of the Great Plains. Baltimore: The Johns Hopkins University Press, 1984.

Pyle, Robert Michael. The Audubon Society Handbook for Butterfly Watchers. New York: Charles Scribner's Sons, 1984.

Scott, James A. The Butterflies of North America: A Natural History and Field Guide. Stanford, Calif.: Stanford University Press, 1986.

Stokes, Donald W. and Lillian Q. Stokes. The Hummingbird Book. Boston: Little, Brown & Company, 1989.

Tekulsky, Mathew. The Butterfly Garden. Boston: Harvard Common Press, 1985.

Tekulsky, Mathew. The Hummingbird Garden. New York: Crown Publishers, Inc., 1990.

Tilden, James W. and Arthur Clayton Smith. A Field Guide to Western Butterflies. Boston: Houghton Mifflin Company, 1986.

Tyrrell, Esther Q. and Robert A. Tyrrell. Hummingbirds. New York: Crown Publishers, Inc., 1985.

Xerces Society/Smithsonian Institution. Butterfly Gardening: Creating Summer Magic in Your Garden. San Francisco: Sierra Club Books, 1990.

Climate Zone Map

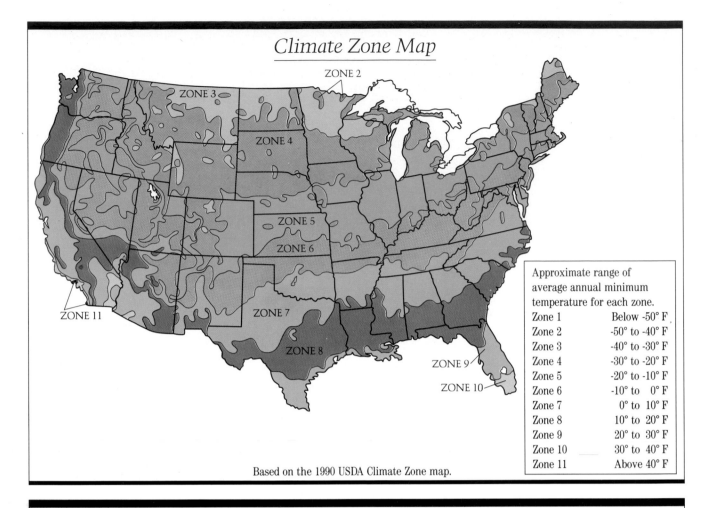

Approximate range of average annual minimum temperature for each zone.

Zone	Temperature
Zone 1	Below -50° F
Zone 2	-50° to -40° F
Zone 3	-40° to -30° F
Zone 4	-30° to -20° F
Zone 5	-20° to -10° F
Zone 6	-10° to 0° F
Zone 7	0° to 10° F
Zone 8	10° to 20° F
Zone 9	20° to 30° F
Zone 10	30° to 40° F
Zone 11	Above 40° F

Based on the 1990 USDA Climate Zone map.

U.S. Measure and Metric Measure Conversion Chart

	Symbol	When you know:	Multiply by:	To find:	Rounded Measures for Quick Reference		
Mass (Weight)	oz	ounces	28.35	grams	1 oz		= 30 g
	lb	pounds	0.45	kilograms	4 oz		= 115 g
	g	grams	0.035	ounces	8 oz		= 225 g
	kg	kilograms	2.2	pounds	16 oz	= 1 lb	= 450 g
					32 oz	= 2 lb	= 900 g
					36 oz	= 2¼ lb	= 1000g (1 kg)
Volume	pt	pints	0.47	liters	1 c	= 8 oz	= 250 ml
	qt	quarts	0.95	liters	2 c (1 pt)	= 16 oz	= 500 ml
	gal	gallons	3.785	liters	4 c (1 qt)	= 32 oz	= 1 liter
	ml	milliliters	0.034	fluid ounces	4 qt (1 gal)	= 128 oz	= 3¾ liter
Length	in.	inches	2.54	centimeters	⅜ in.	= 1 cm	
	ft	feet	30.48	centimeters	1 in.	= 2.5 cm	
	yd	yards	0.9144	meters	2 in.	= 5 cm	
	mi	miles	1.609	kilometers	2½ in.	= 6.5 cm	
	km	kilometers	0.621	miles	12 in. (1 ft)	= 30 cm	
	m	meters	1.094	yards	1 yd	= 90 cm	
	cm	centimeters	0.39	inches	100 ft	= 30 m	
					1 mi	= 1.6 km	
Temperature	°F	Fahrenheit	⅝ (after subtracting 32)	Celsius	32°F	= 0°C	
	°C	Celsius	⅝ (then add 32)	Fahrenheit	212°F	= 100°C	
Area	in.²	square inches	6.452	square centimeters	1 in.²	= 6.5 cm²	
	ft²	square feet	929.0	square centimeters	1 ft²	= 930 cm²	
	yd²	square yards	8361.0	square centimeters	1 yd²	= 8360 cm²	
	a.	acres	0.4047	hectares	1 a.	= 4050 m²	

Formulas for Exact Measures